Making LAW

Making LAW

A MEMOIR of GOOD TIMES

RICHARD C. CAHN

gatekeeper press
Columbus, Ohio

Making Law: A Memoir of Good Times

Published by Gatekeeper Press
2167 Stringtown Rd, Suite 109
Columbus, OH 43123-2989
www.GatekeeperPress.com

Copyright © 2020 by Richard C. Cahn
All rights reserved. Neither this book, nor any parts within it may be sold or reproduced in any form or by any electronic or mechanical means, including information storage and retrieval systems without permission in writing from the author. The only exception is by a reviewer, who may quote short excerpts in a review.

The cover design, interior formatting, typesetting, and editorial work for this book are entirely the product of the author. Gatekeeper Press did not participate in and is not responsible for any aspect of these elements.

ISBN (hardcover): 9781642379518
ISBN (paperback): 9781642379501
eISBN: 9781642379525

CONTENTS

Foreword 9

Goodbye, Sputnik; I'm on my Way Back To 1799 15
Lawyer Cahn's Wild Ride 31
"ALL RISE!" 42
The Army Botches Coeducation 52
Who Will Take Care of Baby Jane Doe? 72
Tilting at Windmills 88
There's a Murderer Out There.
    The Government Doesn't Care. 116
Did a Computer System named MERS
    Destroy the World Economy? 151
Discrimination and the Zoning Laws:
    What is the "Character of the Community"
    We are Preserving? 169
Climate Change 204

Acknowledgments 213
Notes 219

To Michael, Lisa, Dan and Sara,

Thank you for always making your father feel like he was doing something worthwhile. I hope you were right.

—and—

To Vivian,

I traveled this road with you and that has made all the difference.

I love you all!

FOREWORD

I practiced law in good times, fighting good battles. I miss those times because I came to know and respect the Law and it gave me some real chances to influence what was happening in our country. I once thought I might be a journalist or a professor. The reason I chose law was that I wanted to do things more than to teach or report about them.

And, for better or worse, I did.

The six stories I'd like to tell you were special experiences in an exciting 60-year legal career, quite different from what I expected when I left the Justice Department in Washington to practice with my father on Long Island. All of these stories involved important court cases, not just for the people involved in them, but on a larger stage, where my clients and I might "make law" for many more people to come. It was interesting, the way each of them played out, and in most of them, it was exhilarating. Each one was worth fighting, and like most battles, presented an opportunity to reflect upon lessons learned.

At first in my new suburban law practice, the usual legal "matters" presented themselves: wills, house closings, divorce cases—just what any small-town practitioner would expect; necessary, but not particularly challenging. I wanted an opportunity to develop the trial lawyer skills that I admired and hoped to master.

So I was happy when I was asked to defend the Town of Huntington in my first significant litigation case; I wanted to impress my new client with my skills. I soon discovered, however, that, under the law in New York as it then was, the town could not win. Figuring out how to handle that situation involved me in research not only here, but, of all places, across the Atlantic Ocean in the archives of the English House of Lords. A few months later, I nervously stood up for the first time in New York's Court of Appeals, asked its seven judges to abandon a long line of legal authority that they had reaffirmed many times over the years, and explained why I thought it was the proper thing to do. The argument that day unfolded something like a law school class, but not as confrontational as the one John Houseman led years later as the law professor in *The Paper Chase*. I was participating in an important debate; the judges challenged me with respect and civility; and in every way but the result, it was a wonderful experience for any lawyer to have in a maiden appearance before his state's highest court.

I didn't win that appeal, but out of the experience came a belief that lawyers and judges are partners in a worthy enterprise, caring about the Law, and honing and on occasion changing it so as to make it a more effective instrument of fairness and justice. I was very young and inexperienced, but I was on my way to making law.

My way of expressing that may be viewed by some as youthful idealism, and a little surprising, coming from someone of my age. But while writing this book, I realized that, despite having seen so many of the flaws in the legal system, I still retained my hopes and expectations for it.

Part of the reason is that I have seen enough justice done in hard cases—some in this book—to cancel out the unhappy expe-

MAKING LAW

riences where the opposite occurred—also, in some of my cases. What I had thought would be a "small-town law practice" turned out to be neither typical nor small. The more challenging a case was, and the more significant the issues it raised, the greater the possible victory—and the more devastating the possible defeat!

I want to share with you my joy and pride in participating in the American justice system during my 60 years. I hope I can convince you that, so long as that system performs as intended as an independent arbiter, and commands wide respect, it will continue to be a more important protector of our individual rights than any other part of the government. At the end of the book, I will tell you of my concerns—and hope they will be yours, as well—about current political activities that threaten that system and the rule of law upon which it is based, without which our democracy cannot endure.

In these six cases, key participants exercised their rights or performed their duties with our legal traditions very much in mind. Ordinary citizens pitted themselves against federal, state or local officials. They knew they had the right to take the government to court, and felt that they had a fair shot at winning.

I ended up with a large number of cases where someone was accusing public officials of acting improperly. The people who were suing believed they knew what they were entitled to under the Constitution, but the officials on the receiving end of the legal papers had a dramatically different perspective. Important issues were at stake, and there were strongly opposing views. Our Constitution and tradition of justice for all made it possible to resolve our conflicting ideas. Participating in that process produced some great adventures!

In half of the cases in this book, I represented the government, and in the other half, citizens. You can classify them as "David v Goliath" cases (Goliath being the government), but in one, where I represented a county official being sued, the other side was Goliath and contrary to the Biblical tale, Goliath won.

These were all cases that the courts were designed over two hundred years ago to hear. They attracted a lot of attention because they raised questions that had to be addressed, and no part of government other than the court system looked like it was going to address them.

The courts where I was arguing them could set aside a national, state or local policy, or decide a case the other way and legitimize the government's enforcement of it. Some basic rules under which we live were at issue, and the outcome was uncertain. When the judges— unelected ones in the federal courts—sorted them out, there would be widespread repercussions, so the cases attracted great interest. They made many headlines and were reported on radio news programs in faraway places.

History and tradition played a large role in many of my cases, not just the ones I write about here. For 25 years, I represented a very old body called the Trustees of the Freeholders and Commonalty of the Town of Southampton. It was created by a "Royal Patent" issued in 1686 by Thomas Dongan, Governor of the Colony of New York, in the name of King James II of England. The Dongan Patent granted to the Trustees the right to hold and control all the waters and underwater lands in that town—a power that they retain to this day. In that capacity, I pored over musty books of trustee resolutions and communications, maps and deeds, to better defend the Trustees' present-day efforts to protect Southampton's precious natural resources.

Ancient documents were critical in some of those cases. The outcome of an ongoing 21st Century litigation looks at this writing like it may hinge upon a handwritten 1712 document that Eric Shultz, the Trustees' president, found in the dank basement of Southampton Town Hall; it had been carefully preserved for more than 300 years by a succession of town clerks, and although fragile, it was still readable.

MAKING LAW

Traditional legal research (as contrasted with historical research), is a necessary part of preparation for every litigation case, and to me it was a special experience. When I read from the open law books scattered on a library table, it was as if I was entering into a dialogue with lawyers and judges—and other characters who appeared in those books—who had in some cases lived and died 100 years before I was born, but who had now come back to life through these writings to share their ideas and concerns—and their history—with me. These were not just old stale court decisions, written in archaic English; they were living documents conveying to me the customs and understandings of a former time and place, equipping me to better place a present-day dispute into its proper perspective for myself and the judges who would hear it. In one of the six cases in this book, I stood up in Washington and presented arguments solidly grounded in our Constitution and history to the United States Supreme Court.

The tradition and ethos of the legal profession have thus far preserved the rule of law in our nation. They are not widely-known or properly appreciated. A good starting point is to reflect upon the often misinterpreted line from Shakespeare's *Henry the Sixth*, Part II, Act IV, Scene 2: *"The first thing we do, let's kill all the lawyers."* That is an excellent prescription—to invite the coming of tyranny.

We owe a great deal to honest, fair, and courageous judges, who do not act as "politicians with robes," and to lawyers who do not shirk from the duty that representation of a client has imposed upon them, even if they are called upon to challenge powerful forces arrayed against them. I am proud to have been part of that tradition.

These stories show how the rule of law operated during the second half of the twentieth century, touching real people involved in complicated moral and legal conflicts. One involves a triple murder case that cried out for prosecution that no one wanted to initiate, another involves a little war against the United States Army that you probably don't know about, and a third involves a

RICHARD C. CAHN

little document that played a significant role in bringing about the 2007-2008 world economic meltdown. I don't want to include any more spoilers here.

I have given you the names of most of the lawyers, judges and litigants involved in these cases, but in several instances, I changed a name to respect someone's privacy.* But the stories are all true.

I hope you thoroughly enjoy all of them, as I did while living through them, every step of the way!

---

* The first place a changed name appears, I'll indicate that with an asterisk.

1

GOODBYE, SPUTNIK; I'M ON MY WAY BACK TO 1799

On October 4, 1957, the day Sputnik circled the globe, I joined my father to form a law firm in the small town of Huntington, New York, and I was not happy about it.

I had just finished a year as a trial lawyer in the Department of Justice in Washington, D.C. I was one of 44 men and women recruited under Attorney General Herbert Brownell's new recruitment program for honor law graduates, following my graduation from Yale Law School.

I wanted to stay in Washington. I liked working for the public, and I could not think of any more exciting place to do that work. I had just turned 25 that June. I was an unknown minion in the administration of President Eisenhower, but because of my great admiration for him, I felt that I was doing very special work.

My life had momentarily intersected with Eisenhower's when he appeared at my Dartmouth graduation four years before to receive an honorary degree, an occasion that was later viewed as historic because of what he did that day.

The president was expected to rise to express his appreciation and to deliver a homily to the members of the Class of '53 about our hard work and good fortune that had led to the

RICHARD C. CAHN

Dartmouth degree we were about to receive, and the obligations that it imposed upon us; but then, without consulting with political advisors, he added powerful remarks that came to be known as his "Don't Join the Bookburners" speech, his first public shot in a behind-the-scenes battle that ultimately brought down Senator Joseph McCarthy. How he had come to make those comments was not publicly known. I researched the question decades later and learned about a conversation that had taken place on the platform that morning between Eisenhower and two other honorary degree recipients, Judge Joseph Proskauer, a highly respected New York appeals judge, and John J. McCloy, who was the American High Commissioner in post-war Germany.

As we all filed in, in our caps and gowns, Proskauer raised with the president how McCarthy's aides Roy Cohn and G. David Shine were intimidating American embassy personnel overseas into removing books by "suspected Communists" from their libraries, a matter that was becoming a serious concern for our diplomats. Eisenhower, giving no indication that he was well aware of the issue and was already displeased with the way his Secretary of State John Foster Dulles was handling it, said that perhaps he'd "find a way" to speak about the issue in the near future. Proskauer's response was classic: "If you are going to speak about bookburning, Mr. President, there is no better time and place to do it than here and now, in front of this great library." He was referring to the lawn of Dartmouth's Baker Library where the ceremonies were being held before an overflow crowd.

Eisenhower sat back, apparently to mull over what had been said, and shortly thereafter rose to deliver the remarks that would be in the headlines the next morning: "Don't join the Book Burners," he said:

> Don't think you are going to conceal faults
> by concealing evidence that they ever existed.

> Don't be afraid to go in your library and read every book, as long as that document does not offend your ideas of decency. That should be the only censorship.

I had begun to notice and think about what was happening in national politics four years before, when I arrived on the campus. As a freshman, I joined the staff of *The Dartmouth*, the campus daily newspaper which first began publication in 1839; it claimed the title of "The Oldest College Newspaper in America." Its editors during my years had strong liberal views, which unsettled me a little, at first. My father was a long-time conservative Republican, and—to the extent I thought about it in high school—I figured I must be one, myself.

But as I left for college in the fall of 1949, McCarthy began to dominate the national news. The Associated Press teletype machine in *The Dartmouth* office kept us regularly informed of his increasingly strident accusations. I spent a lot of time in that office and made it a point to read well-written and persuasive editorials written by the paper's successive editors-in-chief, notably, Frank Gilroy, an extraordinarily talented writer who went on to win a Pulitzer Prize for his play, "The Subject Was Roses;" and Franklin "Ted" Laskin, who became a lawyer and liberal activist, representing the ACLU in a number of cases. On the pages of the paper, they condemned the loyalty oaths then being required of state university professors in the Midwest and the evil of the "separate but equal" doctrine, before anyone had heard about Brown v Board of Education.

I still identified myself a Republican, but began to wonder how deep my conservative views ran. When Eisenhower, a decent and principled man but not exactly a "true" conservative, came upon the scene, I was delighted, and when he won the nomination for president, I enthusiastically supported him. In the fall of 1952 I wrote a front-page "dissenting opinion" for *The Dartmouth* explaining why eight of the nine editors of the paper (I was Managing Editor by then) disagreed with the decision of Brock Brower, that year's Editor-in-Chief, to have the paper support Stevenson; we liked Ike. That led to Brock and me being invited to participate on opposite sides of a debate before the senior class in a pre-election session of Dartmouth's "Great Issues" course, a political debut for both of us.

Added to those experiences were some of my other assignments for the paper: I spent a full day traveling around the State with New Hampshire Republican Senator Charles Tobey, to all appearances a reserved New England public servant. I tried to capture the human being behind his image, and wrote a long, favorable piece about him that ran on two successive days. I interviewed New Hampshire Governor Sherman Adams, and asked him whether he would support Eisenhower (he did, and became Ike's Chief of Staff in the White House), and Senator "Mike" Monroney, a moderate Democrat from Oklahoma; he and I later exchanged letters about the best way to deal with McCarthyism.

My years at Yale Law School that followed sharpened my understanding of the relationship of law, politics and government toward each other. I loved my weekly class in "Law and Public Opinion" at Mory's, across York Street from the law school, with Professor Fred Rodell, one of the era's foremost legal firebrands, whom I admired forever thereafter. When he died years later, he was remembered as a man who had made a giant impression on the legal world, who "to the very end," was "joyously unrepentant of the idols he had smashed and the great reputations he had sought to puncture."

It was impossible to witness the events of those years without reacting strongly. My classmates and I watched the Army-McCarthy hearings in 1954 on a small black and white television set in the law school dining room. In the summer of the next year, while clerking for the U.S. Attorney's Office in Manhattan, I went to the Second Circuit courtroom on the 21st floor of the U.S. Courthouse and observed members of the House Un-American Activities Committee bullying a number of subpoenaed Hollywood writers and performers, to disclose their political and personal associations and activities. One by one the witnesses uttered magic words written out on a small strip of paper, invoking their Fifth Amendment rights—a single sentence that instantly destroyed their careers—and a wife or girlfriend burst into tears and ran from the courtroom. I wondered how anyone could sit and observe what I saw that day and not see how wrong it was. I thought the Committee had an appropriate name—for its own activities.

Years later, I was sorry to learn that I had missed the appearance of young musician Pete Seeger, who "dissed" the committee members and their attorney. After refusing to say whether he had performed at a meeting in the Bronx of "the Allerton Section [of the Communist Party]," or at other meetings of its members or sympathizers, Seeger said he would "be glad to tell you what songs I have sung, because singing is my business," but thought it was "improper" to ask him "who I have sung them to, especially under such compulsion as this." When asked about a particular song, Seeger politely told them they had the title wrong, but said "I can sing it. I don't know how well I can do it [here] without my banjo … I have never refused to sing for anybody." Seeger effectively took an entirely different legal tack from the witnesses I had seen by invoking his *First* Amendment right not to be questioned about his "associations and opinions." That courageous act—right on the mark legally—brought him years of unpleasant litigation, but he finally won dismissal of the contempt of Congress charges the committee brought against him. But what I saw on the day I attended was bad enough. I left the hearing room telling myself, "I have to get into politics." A year later I was happy to go to the Justice Department for my new job in the nation's capital.

That job was one of those indispensable "nuts and bolts" assignments that introduce a new lawyer to the "how" of law practice, as contrasted with the "what" and the "why" that we concentrated on in law school. I was assigned to the Frauds Section of the Civil Division and asked to review investigative files on potential False Claims Act cases and report to Fred Curley, our Section Chief, whether I thought we had sufficient evidence that the individuals or companies under investigation had cheated the government by falsely certifying they had provided the goods and services they had agreed to supply under a government contract. If we sued them and won, a federal court would order the defendants to pay the government double its damages plus $2,000 for each false claim. Those penalties have substantially increased in the years since.

I began to learn how the FBI worked by reading "302s," the reports by agents of witness interviews. My first assignment was to study 302s on a midwestern meat-packing company that was suspected of providing substandard hamburgers for the Department of Agriculture's school lunch program. After I read the program's detailed specifications for hamburger meat, I put a pull-down chart on the wall of my office that looked just like the "Map of the World" that hung in front of the blackboard in my third-grade classroom, only this one was entitled, "Map of the Cow." Without it, I couldn't quite remember where its various acceptable parts (loin, flank, rib, etc.) were located. There were a lot of laughs when I put it up.

After I returned from my State Bar admission ceremony in New York, Curley asked me to "second seat" my office-mate Maurice Meyer, for the upcoming trial of a case against Florida real estate brokers who were accused of submitting papers to the Veterans Administration to make it falsely appear that qualified veterans were applying for GI mortgages which were subsidized by the government. I roamed the Miami waterfront for several days before the trial with two FBI agents to track down and take statements from veterans who had been coaxed into signing paperwork for a home they never intended to buy. They were sad men, homeless derelicts, and many appeared to be alcoholics—all clearly victims of the scheme, as was the U.S. Government. In my later years in private practice, I prepared for many trials without the help of any FBI agents, and I missed them. They were a hard act to follow.

During my year in Washington, I walked up Pennsylvania Avenue to the Supreme Court and heard arguments by first-rate lawyers. On a few occasions I sat in the visitors' galleries in the Senate and House of Representatives, hoping—often in vain—to witness a good debate about an important public issue. My friends were working in Justice, or in another department or agency, or in Congress, and on many days, over drinks after work, our conversation turned towards the political "buzz" of the day. Life inside the future Beltway was vibrant and exciting.

But, having by the summer of 1957 spent almost a year there, I was being pressed by my father to return to Long Island to be the "junior partner" of Cahn & Cahn. He had talked about our being future law partners from my first days in law school. I loved and respected my father, but he had long been a formidable presence in my life and the thought of practicing law with him was intimidating. I hoped I could find a gracious way out, and for a few months I put off my decision. I was excited to learn that an attractive position might shortly open up in the small but prestigious Office of Legal Counsel in the Justice Department, which in those days served as counsel to a single client, the President of the United States. But the job failed to materialize.

I finally told my dad I would return to Long Island and sent the new Attorney General William Rogers my letter of resignation. I tried to believe that exciting opportunities would present themselves to me back in Huntington, although that seemed unlikely. But I would give it a try.

Before leaving Washington, I took steps to keep my political options alive, such as they might be, by going to the West Wing of the White House to visit Sherman Adams, the former New Hampshire governor whom I had interviewed several years before for *The Dartmouth*. Adams was still called "Governor," and was then President Eisenhower's Chief of Staff. He welcomed me to his office and gave me a letter of introduction to Leonard Hall, the former Republican National Chairman who had returned to private law practice in Oyster Bay, the town next to Huntington. That got me started in Suffolk County politics.

Immediately after I returned to Long Island, the news about Sputnik broke and my sense of despair deepened. The country would now be gearing up to challenge the Russians in space; major projects were ahead, many new government jobs would be created, and there would probably be unusual challenges for young lawyers to solve—perhaps even helping to write "Space Law!" Washington was about to become even more exciting, and I had just left all that behind. Goodbye, Sputnik!

I was sure now that even if I could navigate a new relationship with my father, I would be suffocated in a small-town law practice. But a case soon came to me that made me think that my death by suffocation might not be inevitable.

After I settled into our office in a very old building in which the musty smell of its second-floor hallway competed with the antiseptic scent of an adjacent dental office—smells that made me worry about suffocation again—I was asked to defend the case of Berg v. Town of Huntington, which looked like a run-of-the-mill one-car accident case, but wasn't.

The woman behind the wheel was not a licensed driver, and there was evidence that she was under the influence of alcohol.

The car failed to navigate a sharp curve and struck a tree, and her three-year-old daughter riding in the back seat was badly injured. The child's father sued the town for his daughter's injuries, claiming that the car skidded off the road on loose gravel that the town spread during the winter and never cleared. The town was the only defendant and I was its lawyer.

Despite the mother's culpability, no one had sued her, which was not surprising considering that the case was brought by her husband. Because of an ancient rule, I had no way to bring her into the case and make her (or her insurance company) take on at least some of that responsibility. The jury would be sympathetic to the child's plight and would have no one other than the town against whom to render a verdict. As I researched the case, I realized we would not escape liability unless we could find a way "to make law."

"Making law" is a euphemism used by generations of lawyers who realize that their client's cause, no matter how just, is probably doomed unless they can pull the lawyer's equivalent of a rabbit out of a hat, by finding a way to break free from adverse precedent created by earlier court decisions.

The New York courts had long ago prohibited "contribution among tortfeasors," meaning that one wrongdoer could not lessen its own financial exposure by forcing another wrongdoer to contribute to the payment of the injured party's claim. The only way the town could bring Mrs. Berg into the case and pass on to her any part of the responsibility for the crash would be to persuade New York's courts to abandon the rule.

I had planned to go to London in the summer of 1959 for a six-week program in English Law. I thought that the use of the language by English judges was magnificent, whether they were speaking from the bench while wearing their gray wigs or crafting their written decisions for the law books. I heard them deliver some of those extemporaneous oral decisions that summer while watching trials at the "Old Bailey," London's Central Criminal Court.

I couldn't stop thinking about the Berg case. I was going to argue it that fall in my first appearance before New York's highest court. I walked into the University of London's law library to look into the history of the "no contribution" rule, which had originated in England. There was nothing unusual about the rule having found its way into New York law. English law is the foundation of American common law and applies in all of our states except Louisiana.

The rule originated in a 1799 decision of the House of Lords in a case called Merryweather v Nixon, but there in the library in London I found a case called Palmer v Wick & Pultneytown Steam Shipping Co., decided in 1884, in which the House of Lords refused to extend the rule to Scotland, even though it had been embedded in English law for 85 years. Lord Herschell made plain that he and his current colleagues thought that the "no contribution" rule was a bad one; they did not believe it was "founded on any principle of justice or equity, or even of public policy."

I had found a good example of a prestigious court effectively abandoning a precedent that it had created itself and adhered to for many years. And it was the very precedent that governed the Berg case.

That October, stressing the fundamental unfairness of the rule, I did argue the case in Albany, and as I had hoped, the judges, particularly Judge Stanley Fuld, were clearly interested. I wondered whether he was just impressed by my demonstration of *chutzpah*, asking his Court to overrule what was by then a 150-year-old precedent of the venerable House of Lords and create a whole new rule for tort liability in New York.

Despite their obvious interest in the case, Judge Fuld and all of his colleagues voted to dismiss the town's claim against Mrs.

Berg. There would still be "no contribution among tortfeasors" in New York; the rule would not change. Not yet.

The judges had asked me a lot of questions, and it seemed to me that Judge Fuld and two of his colleagues had been willing to seriously consider changing the rule. I wondered how close I came to convincing them.

Notwithstanding losing the appeal, I felt I had done something worthwhile. I had stood before the state's highest court and asked its judges to change an unjust rule that had hurt many people for many years and had outlived any legitimate purpose. And the judges were listening to me! I realized that in my role as a trial lawyer I could plant ideas, which possibly, in time, might ripen into actual change.

I was happy to see the issue come back in 1972, in a case called Dole v. Dow Chemical Company. This time, the Court—Judge Fuld was now its Chief—did abolish the "no contribution" rule, as I had asked it to do 13 years before. The judges wrote that there was "widespread dissatisfaction" with the rule's "inequity," and now agreed that "the deciding factor should be fairness as between the parties." I will never know whether my argument in 1959 had actually influenced the judges when they finally decided the question, but it is nice to speculate about it.

Berg made me rethink my concern about being trapped in a "small-town" law practice. It, and then the Dole case, taught me that some of the country's great public policy cases, including many that reached a state's highest court or perhaps the Supreme Court, had started in somebody's small-town law practice, and that often a "small-town" lawyer—perhaps one like me—would first identify an important issue at stake and persuade a trial judge—sitting in the first tier of the nation's courts—that the case could not be fairly decided without addressing it. Extremely important things were happening at the lowest level of the court system, often out of the public's sight and mind.

I knew that in the future, even in my "small-town" practice, I could be involved in shaping the Law, an exciting possibility. I hadn't yet reached the level of cynicism of Fred Rodell. He had viewed judges, as *The Nation* said, "as no more than politicians in robes using legalistic mumbo-jumbo to write their politics into law." But I began to realize that Rodell was right about one thing: the court system where I was plying my trade was, in fact, dealing in politics. But, unlike Rodell (or, his reputation, anyway!), I had the notion that in cases where fairness or justice required that the law or public policy be changed, judges could properly change them without becoming "politicians with robes." And I, practicing before those judges, could help legitimatize that process.

So, my interest in politics, which had initially brought me to the nation's capital, ironically took the form of activity in the court system, which conventional wisdom dictated should be politics-free.

My respect for that system started with great respect for the character and dedication of the lawyers and judges who made the system work. My first example was my father, who influenced me in many ways.

For many years, he was an aggressive and articulate warrior. Those traits were an extension of his strong personality that I knew from my growing-up years. Those who had not been exposed to him never expected a man barely five-six in height and weighing 135 pounds to dominate a courtroom as he did. Our family knew he had been an amateur prize-fighter in his youth, and that he could be aggressive. People who did not know his background were startled to see this physically diminutive man command a courtroom so effectively. His best weapons there were not his fists, but his encyclopedic knowledge of the English language and his ability to use it so precisely that hostile witnesses could never escape the logical conclusions that would be drawn from the admissions that he had forced from their lips. I saw lawyers sitting in the back of courtrooms where he was performing, learning from him; one told me he was "a master." When I watched him, I remembered the times during my years at home when I had been the victim of those same techniques in—how shall I say it delicately—one of our disciplinary encounters.

But, as I indicated, an equally important part of my father's reputation had to do with his insistence upon ethical behavior. More than one of his colleagues told me, "You never needed a written stipulation with Irving; his word was his bond." That was true; he never forgot what he had promised, or failed to honor a commitment, and he expected the same of everyone else. One of the first pieces of advice he gave me, was "You should trust a lawyer's word when you first meet him, but if he betrays your trust, mark him lousy forever."

There was a soft side to him. My most tender memory of my father is of the time I was hospitalized at the age of six for hip surgery and then immobilized at home in a full-body plaster cast. I can still remember how good it felt, when my dad, a small man, lovingly carried the 80 or so pounds of me up and down stairs every day for six months. That simple but physically taxing act, repeated uncomplainingly so often, has long outweighed my memories of his occasional withering outbursts of fury.

Although he could be gracious and affable, he could instantly turn hostile if his judgment or knowledge were challenged or questioned, or if someone belittled his physical size or demeaned our family background. I was present for a conference in the chambers of a judge who was presiding over a murder case that my father was defending. In front of the jury, the assistant district attorney repeatedly referred to my father as "Little Man," to which my father snapped back some equally nasty rejoinder. The judge finally lost patience and ordered the lawyers into his chambers, at which point the prosecutor hit my father's second hot button and made a reference to him as "this little Jew." Immediately, my father seized a heavy glass ashtray and prepared to smash it against the man's head, failing to connect only because a court officer hurled his body between the two men. His Honor James L. Dowsey, Jr., the mild-mannered judge, sitting at the far end of the conference table, put his hands over his face and, over and over again, repeated "Oh dear, oh dear, oh dear."

He never tried to brain me, but he could be so intimidating that even when I knew for a fact that he was wrong, it was impossible for me to summon the courage to contradict him. The feeling lingered into adulthood, and now we were going to be law partners.

Upon my return to Huntington in 1957, my father decided to work initially out of his existing office 20 miles away in adjacent Nassau County while I staffed the new office in Huntington. I was relieved not to have him looking over my shoulder all day long, and to discover that I would have virtually complete autonomy to develop a practice that would suit my preferences, and to handle it without draconian supervision.

But there were many opportunities to make my own mistakes, and I still needed to consult with him. On one embarrassing occasion, I roundly cursed out the Bronx County sheriff after he informed me that he would take five percent "poundage" from the money he seized at my request from a debtor's bank account for the benefit of my client, to whom the money was owed. I had never in my life heard of "poundage," but was uneasy about my own outburst and called my father at the other office. He was silent for a few seconds, and then clued me in on what was an English method of compensating sheriffs. My not knowing about it wasn't excusable; it was not some addition to the law books that was so recent that it escaped my notice: New York had adopted it more than 200 years before, shortly after the American Revolution. I swallowed hard and called the sheriff back to apologize; for all I knew, he was a perfectly honest city official. He laughed and told me he got calls like mine at least three times a week: "Don't worry about it, counselor," he said.

When my father and I later began to work together in the same office, our relationship became dramatically different; we brainstormed new cases, exchanging ideas as colleagues, and when the time came to prepare briefs for the courts, we fell into an unusual routine: he or I would dictate the first paragraphs to our secretary, one of a handful of talented women who through the years faithfully took our words down in shorthand. Then the other one of us would pick up the narrative. It was as though we shared a single legal mind from which the ultimate work product sprang. When our briefs were typed up, neither of us could remember which of us had authored each part.

After we had done that a few times, I was no longer in doubt; he respected my ability and judgment. I had pleased him. I had arrived.

Less than four years after I returned from Washington, he had a heart attack, went to Florida, became incapacitated for most of the next four years, and then, sadly, died at 63, cruelly cutting short the career to which he had devoted his life and for which he was widely admired, sometimes in unexpected circles. He had defended a lot of criminal cases, and had cross-examined many Nassau County police officers through the years, thoroughly embarrassing them as they were forced to acknowledge errors they had made in handling an investigation or arrest. None of them took it personally; they genuinely respected and liked him. Some years later, when the police learned that the husband of one of his matrimonial clients (a man he had also harshly cross-examined) had threatened his life, two police officers showed up unannounced at our house in Freeport on a holiday morning when public offices were closed, to drive him to the home of a county judge whose duties included issuing pistol permits. After the judge signed the papers, one of the officers took out his holstered gun and handed it to my father, saying, "Carry this everywhere you go until you get one of your own, Irving. I have a spare." The man who had threatened his life never tried to carry out an attack, but my father carried a gun until he died.

My father's imprint in many ways upon my family—and upon me—was so strong that we imputed things to him that our rational minds knew couldn't be true. During his long illness he said to several family members that once he went to "wherever you go when you die," he would send us a message to let us know he had arrived. "How will we know it's a message from you?" my wife, Vivian, asked him. "Oh, you'll know," he said, "it will be unmistakable." Several hours after his death on November 9, 1965, the great northeastern blackout turned off the lights of 30 million people in the U.S. and Canada.

2

LAWYER CAHN'S WILD RIDE

My 60-year voyage as a trial lawyer through our American justice system was a wild ride for "Lawyer Cahn." That was how Karl Malden referred to me in the TV drama based on one of those cases, and that Michael and Lisa, my oldest children, engraved on a medallion that they had made for me.

It was a good name, I thought. Even while I was in law school, I felt privileged that I would soon become a part of a very old, well-established and highly-regarded legal system with its own special rules and expectations, chief among which was to command lawyers and judges to act honorably and avoid what was usually called "even the appearance of impropriety." From the beginning, I appreciated the value of legal precedent as a consistent and reliable guide for human conduct, but I came to believe, as most lawyers do, that in some cases, consistency would need to yield to justice. I felt that the Law had a humanitarian ingredient, and it was important not to forget it.

Over the years the legal profession took many steps to improve the quality of justice. A major one was taken in the 1963 case of Gideon v. Wainwright, when the Supreme Court required states to provide defense counsel to indigent persons who were charged with crime. That ruling would change the landscape in the nation's criminal courts; lawyers in every part of the country would carry out those new duties. One immediate result in our area was the establishment of the Legal Aid Society in my home county of Suffolk a year later. Actually, in an 1881 law that preceded Gideon by 82 years, New York State had required that counsel be provided for indigent felony defendants, and there was already a well-established assignment tradition when I first arrived in Suffolk. Assigned defense services were performed for a small hourly fee that the State paid, and many lawyers responded. Before Gideon, I had already defended several criminal cases in both the federal and state courts, and I volunteered for defense assignments under the new system.

The year 1963 brought me a major one. Leonard Wexler, an experienced local criminal defense lawyer, and I were asked by the court to defend a man who had been accused of killing three people during an eight-day spree in 1959. The county's residents had been terrified and massive media coverage inflamed their fears. The newspapers tagged him the "Mad Killer," and the trial we agreed to handle would again be covered in the press as the "triple murder case," despite the fact that the trial would be limited to one crime. It would prove to be a challenging assignment.

Our client had been tried and convicted for one of those killings, but the federal Circuit Court set aside the conviction on the ground of jury prejudice. A new trial—to which Wexler and I were assigned—was ordered to take place in Manhattan.

That trial became a living example of what I told my family through the years a lawyer is required to do in criminal cases. At one time or another, each of my children asked me how I could "defend someone who I knew was guilty." I pointed out that I could never "know" for certain whether a client was guilty of a crime, and asked them to "imagine that you have been charged with a crime, and a D.A. was in the process of placing questionable evidence before your jury." They saw, of course, that their interest would clearly lie in having that evidence challenged and tested by their defense lawyer in the strongest possible way. Only if that evidence stood up against a stiff challenge would it be appropriate for them to be punished.

Wexler and I both recognized our duty to provide a strong defense, and we relished the opportunity. We were not only going to have to do whatever we could to ensure that this trial would be fair; we would need to expose to the light of day what clearly looked like egregious misconduct by our predecessor in the case, a prominent Suffolk County lawyer. He had coaxed his client, who was now ours, to confess to the crimes, when he had a glaring conflict of interest in the form of a powerful personal motive to "deliver" a high-value criminal defendant to the prosecutors: at the very time he was advising his client to confess, serious criminal charges were pending against the lawyer himself. And, lo and behold, when the client followed his advice, the charges against his lawyer were dismissed. There was no way that Wexler and I believed that those two events were unconnected.

Wexler prepared to intensely cross-examine the former lawyer (who, ironically, had been his first boss), and also the former District Attorney who had dismissed the charges against him. Wexler learned later that the Circuit judges in Manhattan who had set aside the earlier conviction were so concerned about what had happened in Suffolk County and might happen again that they sent a monitor to watch the second trial to assure themselves that the new lawyers in the case were performing properly. Neither Wexler nor I had any idea at the time that we were being surveilled as we tried the case. The monitor later told the judges that he had no concerns.

While my co-counsel was preparing for those explosive witness examinations, I took charge of a separate attack we wanted to make on our client's confession. By means of isolation, threats of violence, and almost certainly one or more actual beatings at the hands of the police—not to mention his former lawyer's advice—he had come to confess to these crimes. I learned that Dr. Joost Meerloo, a world-famous Dutch psychiatrist who had researched and written about "mental coercion," later called "brainwashing," was then living on Central Park West in New York City. I called him, and he invited me to visit him there.

That visit put me in touch with history. Meerloo had studied how the Nazis had extracted a confession in the Reichstag fire case in 1933 from a young unemployed Dutch bricklayer named Marinus van der Lubbe, using techniques that Joseph Stalin adopted several years later in his "Great Purge" of thousands of Soviet citizens whom he considered threats to his power.

Meerloo was a charming man. He was happy to answer my questions about the Van Der Lubbe case over tea at his apartment, and I could have spent a great deal more time listening. At some point, however, we turned to the case at hand, and it was his turn to listen as I outlined what I knew so far of our client's treatment at the hands of the police and prosecutors—and his own lawyer. Meerloo began to think out loud, organizing in his mind and mine the elements of our case that made a persuasive case that the confession was the product of mental coercion. He agreed to become our principal witness, and with his help, we would try to keep that confession from the jury. After the trial, we learned that the jury was extremely impressed with Meerloo, considering him far more credible than the prosecution's psychiatrist, but nonetheless the confession was admitted in evidence.

Several years after that trial, I got two brief tastes of life as a prosecutor, first joining the District Attorney's office as acting head of the appeals bureau, and then becoming a special prosecutor in a homicide case, when for the first and only time in my life I presented evidence to a grand jury, and asked the panel to indict two young men for murder. They had decided to "roll" an elderly man drinking in a bar, followed him into the parking lot, struck him on the head with a beer bottle, and took his money. They later said they were "surprised" that the blow had killed him.

One of the defendants was a cousin of the wife of George Aspland, the sitting District Attorney, who—as the ethics rules counselled—recused his entire office from handling that case, so it fell to Gordon Lipetz, the Chief Judge of our County Court, to ask a lawyer independent of the DA's office to prosecute it, and he chose me.

The men were indicted and the defendants initially released on bail pending trial, but when I learned that they were physically threatening several witnesses who would testify against them, I immediately had their bail revoked. Shortly after the trial began, they both pleaded guilty and went to prison.

My short assignment as a special prosecutor was a job I dutifully did, but any joy I had out of the experience derived from working with George Latchford, a tall, curly-haired, handsome and dedicated but fun-loving detective who headed the Homicide Bureau of the Suffolk County Police Department. He had steady determination, it seemed, to solve and meticulously prepare for the trial of every case that came to his bureau. But my strongest memory of George was his quirky sense of humor, which provided a few welcome laughs as we prepared a tawdry murder case for trial.

Working with him reminded me of my time interviewing witnesses on the Miami docks with those FBI agents, years before. I realized again the tremendous advantage prosecutors have over defense lawyers because of the investigative resources at their disposal, which dwarf those available to the usual criminal defendant.

I found matrimonial cases extremely stressful, and stopped handling them after a stunning encounter with one of my former divorce clients. She called me at 2:15 one afternoon "to say goodbye." "Oh," I said, "where are you going?" "I'm not going anywhere," she said; "I'm going to kill myself in 45 minutes." "What?" I blurted out, and then I dredged up from somewhere a question that, in retrospect, could have quickly precipitated the very event I was trying to stop from happening: "Why aren't you doing it now, why are you waiting 45 minutes?"

"Because my daughter is coming home on the school bus at three o'clock and I'm going to kill her first."

I remember the tension as I kept her on the phone for 43 of those 45 minutes, while on another line my secretary frantically tried to direct the police who were having trouble finding the client's house. Barely two minutes before the daughter's school bus was due to arrive, still talking and asking time-filling questions, I heard the client's doorbell ring in the background. She excused herself to go to the door, just as if it were an ordinary day. A minute or so later, a male voice came on the phone: "This is Patrolman____ of the SCPD." Before I could respond, he added, "Counsellor, your client wants to talk to you."

She came on the line.

"*You bastard!*" she said.

Three months later, released from detention and treatment, she, with her daughter, appeared at my office, both fitted out in their most beautiful dresses. All I can remember that she said was "Thank you so much, Richard. I'm sorry." We hugged, and tears came to my eyes.

Some of the civil cases that I was asked to handle were so outlandish that I was amazed that they ever arose. One involved Charles Clark, a former attendant at Pilgrim State Hospital, one of the State's mental hospitals, who himself had been committed for schizophrenia. Because of his disability, he missed the statutory deadline to file for his government pension. It was hard to believe that his supervisor, a psychiatrist, didn't think mental illness was a sufficient excuse for a late filing. I had to sue the New York Comptroller to compel the State to pay him.

I became interested in the work of the Suffolk County Bar Association, an exceptionally forward-looking organization which took an active role in screening candidates for judgeships, and whose officers and directors didn't hesitate to butt heads with administrative judges or other powerful men in the legal establishment (there were not many women in those positions in those days), if rules they handed down seemed inappropriate or unworkable for the practicing bar. The bar association burnished its already superb reputation by forming a separate educational arm, the Suffolk Academy of Law, to establish a program of lectures on a wide variety of legal topics, twenty years before Continuing Legal Education became mandatory for lawyers. In later years, I attended those CLE classes, and on occasion lectured in them.

In the earlier years, I was one of only a few lawyers in our area who practiced in the federal courts, so my interest in the bar association initially revolved around its federal courts committee, which I joined early in my career, eventually becoming its chair and writing a report that resulted in Congress' amending the federal Judiciary Act to allow the federal court in the Eastern District of New York, which had previously held its sessions only in Brooklyn, to sit also in Nassau and Suffolk Counties. Now judges from Long Island sit in a $200 million federal court building in the west end of Suffolk.

One year, I chaired the Bar Association's grievance committee and discovered, both sadly and with relief, that the vast majority of grievances before us were against the same small handful of lawyers, whose names came up again and again. I prosecuted a disciplinary proceeding against Edward Charpentier,* one of the County's best-known criminal lawyers, who had an almost

Shakespearean way with words and was well-liked by his colleagues at the bar—our own loveable rascal. He regularly went into the county jail in Riverhead to visit the latest batch of prisoners, offering to represent each of them for a modest fee and picking up cash from each of them, $25 here and $40 there. The charges against him involved his collecting all that money but then doing no legal work for many of those "clients." I crossed paths with Lenny Wexler again when he appeared as Charpentier's defense counsel.

Charpentier was trying a criminal case in Riverhead when the judge presiding over the trial called him to the bench and gave him the news that the Appellate Division in Brooklyn, the supervising court for disciplinary proceedings, had just ordered him disbarred. Without shedding a tear, he turned away from the judge. "The angels have spoken," he murmured, and he walked out of the courthouse for the last time.

I was elected President of the Bar Association and served in 1981-82. Several months after I was sworn in, I attended my first naturalization ceremony. Several hundred people had gathered in Riverhead, our County seat, to take a far weightier oath—of allegiance to the United States of America—which was to be administered, as was customary, by one of our local judges, this one bearing a quintessentially American name: John J. J. Jones.

The large room was crowded, people everywhere holding small American flags, children on parents' laps, and smiles on every face, mine and Justice Jones included. The noisy courtroom that ordinarily served as the venue for somber judicial proceedings, was transformed. Every place in the many rows of wooden benches was occupied by a man, woman or child who would shortly be a freshly-minted American citizen, a dream come true. The words of the Pledge of Allegiance filled the air in a hundred voices and accents. I was conscious that I was the grandson of immigrants who had taken the same oath 80 years before, as I stepped to the podium to deliver my own welcome to my fellow citizens into the nation that was about to become theirs, too, I believed my words reflected what most Americans would have wanted to be said had they been there that day. I chose to speak about our Constitution and laws and how America's strength derived from the talents and ambition of so many people, just like them, who had seen opportunities, particularly for their children, to thrive in a beautiful country with stable and reliable laws.

That year I also maintained the Bar Association's tradition of outspokenness by publicly tangling with Lawrence H. Cooke, then New York's Chief Judge, on the Letters to the Editor page of the *New York Times*.

Politics was intertwined with law. During the early years, I spent untold hours toting nominating petitions, in court defending ballot positions for Republican candidates, and providing legal advice for party leaders. Other local lawyers in both major parties were doing the same kind of work, hoping to be rewarded eventually with a nomination or an appointment to public office, or a judgeship. And some were.

I do not claim that the system of selecting judges in those days was perfect, or that lawyers, whether they continued to practice or became judges, always acted admirably. To the contrary, lawyers sometimes cut ethical corners, something that was easy to spot but hard for me to deal with, particularly after hearing my father's "mark him lousy" comment for so many years. And judges at all stages of their career could be hostile or disinterested, or just plain self-destructive.

One day a lower court judge I had known from the earlier years when he was a young lawyer in town, sent his court officer out to buy him a cup of coffee from a vendor in the courthouse parking lot. The officer complied, the judge tasted it, declared it "putrid," spat it out, and ordered the court officer to go out again, arrest the coffee vendor and bring him back in handcuffs. Unfortunately for the judge, the officer followed his order. At the end of this uplifting story, the judge was removed from the bench and saw a federal court jury return a $140,000 judgment against him for violating the vendor's civil rights.

To return to a description of normal behavior, relationships in local politics in those days were generally quite different than they are today. Tribal animosity between political adversaries had not yet taken root, and although there were some glaring exceptions, friendly interactions between active members of the two major parties were commonplace; I was not unusual in having as many friendships with Democratic candidates and officeholders as with Republican ones; we had a lot more in common than what divided us.

I was receiving telephone calls from potential clients who figured I had special knowledge about cases against the government. Some wanted to sue a government official and others were themselves town or county officials who needed a defense, and I entered an odd corner of our political world, where people take a grievance against some official or agency to the government's own court. They knew that they could do more than gripe; they could try to change things, and had a fair chance of success. Who said you can't fight city hall?

The facts of the cases varied, but in one form or another they all asked the same question: what limits are there to what our government can (or should) do for, or to us?

In most cases, the trial judge "frames the issues," a task that takes on special significance when the case is one challenging the constitutionality of a law or the legality of an act by a government official. Contrary to my initial assumption that it was only in Congress, the White House, and the highest appeal courts that decisions were being made about the direction and character of the country, long before any of the cases I was beginning to handle could conceivably end up before the Supreme Court, a trial judge somewhere had to make a ruling that would fix the boundaries, not only of what that judge would decide, but also what the appeal courts could decide in the case. Even the Supreme Court will not generally rule on questions that have not been litigated in the lower courts. Thus, an enormous power resided in the trial judges; in numerous ways, large and small, they shaped public policy, sometimes in more meaningful and significant ways than was being done by all of the instrumentalities of government that I saw at work during my year in Washington. But those trial judges would only have the opportunity to exercise that enormous power if the trial lawyers saw the larger questions in a case and litigated them.

No one should minimize the seriousness of representing an individual client in a case that is personally important, although not necessarily so to the general public, but as I became increasingly active in cases that involved public policy, I realized that in some important way they had placed me in a new, expanded, sphere of lawyering, and made me responsible to a much larger group of people.

The cases I handled, including the ones I've written about here, gave me a far deeper understanding of how the justice system was supposed to work and how it worked in real life. The aspirational and the actual were close enough in those years that I retained a deep respect for the system's design and its ability to right wrongs. I never stopped enjoying working with, and learning from, lawyers and judges who did their best to adhere to the profession's high standards.

They were good at what they did.

3
"ALL RISE!"

Those words are intoned every day in thousands of American courtrooms, whether presided over by nine justices of the United States Supreme Court or by a magistrate in a tiny village.

We do rise. I did it for 60 years.

The gesture is meant to express respect for the men and women who wear black robes, and confidence that they will fairly decide the cases presented to them. However, "deciding cases" does not come close to describing the importance of what they do.

The federal courts date back to the original Constitution in 1787, and each state has had its own court system since it was admitted to the Union—and a colonial or territorial court system before that. For all that time, judges, as the federal courts' website puts it, have been "shaping history." Many Supreme Court decisions, going back more than two centuries, have changed the way we relate to one other and to our society's institutions. Since the 1803 Supreme Court case of Marbury v. Madison, the federal courts have wielded impressive power: a single judge can stop the President of the United States from abusing his authority. No party appears in the federal court dockets more than the government itself.

MAKING LAW

The Brennan Center for Justice at New York University points out that the decisions of the state courts, where 95 percent of all cases in the United States are filed, also "touch on virtually every aspect of Americans' lives."

The public for many years has been sharply divided on very important questions, a good many of which ended up in court. Supreme Court decisions in recent times outlawed prayer in public schools, ruled that the Second Amendment guarantees individuals' rights to own firearms, whether or not they are members of the National Guard, today's "militia;" preserved a woman's right to seek an abortion; found that the religious objections of individuals who provide health insurance to their employees are entitled to greater protection than the employees' rights to coverage for birth control and abortion; found that enforcement of voting rights laws is no longer justified in certain states, notwithstanding an earlier history in those places of widespread racial discrimination; and outlawed limitations on political contributions as unconstitutional because they limit protected "speech." The courts have historically taken sides on many hotly-contested "public issues," yet managed to retain the respect of that public.

The six cases I write about here also involved public issues and affected many lives. Before I tell you those stories, I'd like to set the stage by telling you a little more about the often-mystifying profession called "The Law."

That profession is primarily self-regulated. Lawyers organize themselves into bar associations, the pre-eminent of which are the state bar associations and the American Bar Association. For well over a century, since the early 1900s, the ABA has established professional goals and standards for lawyers and judges and drafted rules setting the bounds of permissible professional behavior. Lawyers and judges are required to comply with those rules and are admonished to act in accordance with the profession's highest ideals. If they don't follow the rules, certain designated judges will decide what punishment—potentially including disbarment of a lawyer or removal of a fellow judge from the bench—will be meted out.

The main work of the Bar is the preservation and improvement of an American justice system—actually, parallel systems of federal and state courts that act separately, often toward the same ends. They adhere to the same rules of professional and judicial conduct; value fair and impartial justice; and agree upon various initiatives that promote those ends, such as making legal representation in the criminal and civil courts available to indigents. No one would claim that either system is perfect in the real world, but they subscribe to and promote the same ideals.

In major part because of their dedication to those ideals, the courts are accepted as fair arbiters not only of private disputes but also of conflicts involving passionate disagreement between the two principal political parties over public policies. Courts, state and federal, have acted on many occasions to block policies or "political" actions that violate a specific requirement of the law or of the Constitution.

For the courts to act against the other two branches of government, they must be independent of them. Alexander Hamilton, in *Federalist No. 78*, said plainly that "there is no liberty, if the power of judging be not separated from the legislative and executive powers." He recommended that judges be appointed for life as an additional safeguard of the independence of the courts, which he believed would be "the citadel of the public justice and the public security." He said the courts should be "an intermediate body between the people and the legislature, in order, among other things, to keep the latter within the limits assigned to their authority." James Madison, in *Federalist No 51*, explained why the judicial branch of government was different from the other two: judges had to be selected by a method that "best secures" the "peculiar qualifications" required of them; and they should have permanent tenure, because that would "soon destroy all sense of dependence on the authority" responsible for their appointment.

Hamilton regarded judicial independence as necessary "to guard the Constitution and the rights of individuals [from] the arts of designing men," which tend "to occasion dangerous innovations in the government, and serious oppressions of the minor party in the community." As antiquated as his language is, his sentiments come through loud and clear, and have resonated through the ages.

President Eisenhower, whose "Farewell Address" warning about the dangers of the "Military-Industrial Complex" has been widely quoted and admired, delivered an earlier address, in 1955, warning about the danger to "the independence and integrity and capacity of the judiciary," which are "vital to our nation's continued existence." The danger he was talking about was the politicization of the courts.

The courts' independence is even more important to preserve today because of the increase in cases involving conflicts that are as political as legal.

In 2005, future Justice Neil Gorsuch published an article in the *National Review* endorsing the statement that American liberals had "become addicted to the courtroom, relying on judges and lawyers, rather than elected leaders and the ballot box, as the primary means of effecting their social agenda." Gorsuch, borrowing Rodell's language, seemed to be saying that asking judges to decide political controversies turns them into "politicians with robes," but I disagree with that. Judges only become politicians when their decisions are partisan.

Judges making policy changes used to be called "judicial activists." One of the nation's leading conservative thinkers, George F. Will, regrets that "for many years" conservatives "have unreflectively and imprudently celebrated judicial restraint," and argues that "conservatism has no more urgent task than that of convincing the country that judicial deference is dereliction of duty." To Will, "courts matter in America more than in any other democracy;" it is essential that we have "engaged" judges who will no longer automatically defer to actions of Congress or the president and will set them aside if they infringe on rights specified or implied by the Constitution.

The tradition of challenging government overreach in the courts is now a well-accepted part of the American legal tradition, and partisans on both sides of the nation's political divide will continue to seek redress in the courts against what they perceive to be the excesses of their adversaries. As those cases proliferate, questions about how judges address them will increase. Will they conceive themselves as owing their loyalty to our traditional system of justice, or will they owe it to a political party or faction? It is the latter that converts them into "politicians with robes."

A good part of the reason the judicial system has worked for so long and well is that enough judges and lawyers took the professional rules and traditions governing Bench and Bar seriously enough at least to refrain from overtly invoking political preferences. There was generally a critical mass of people who knew that in every case, there was more at stake than who wins and who loses: the independence, reputation and effectiveness of the court system itself. The public saw that, and respected it.

Justice Anthony Kennedy put it this way: "The law commands allegiance only if it commands respect. It commands respect only if the public thinks the judges are neutral."

Over my years in practice, I encountered judges whose first instinct was not to prejudge a case, even a politically tinged one, but to keep an open mind and listen carefully; they knew that restraint on their part was called for.

Although a judge may be called upon to act immediately (for example, to grant or deny a temporary injunction), normally no immediate action in a case is initially required, and a judge who is so inclined has the luxury of digesting all of the arguments on both sides before deciding anything permanent. Impartial judges are thoughtful and deliberate and give no indication of any hidden agenda, because they have none. There is something intangible but obvious about their demeanor that reassures lawyers on both sides—and their clients—that they can be trusted to decide the case fairly; in Justice Kennedy's words, this is a "neutral" judge. Such judges might seek, carefully, to clarify or even change the law, but it was obvious from their history and reputation as well as their demeanor on the bench that they were doing so not for political reasons, but because fairness seemed to require it.

I also saw many lawyers in action who understood that they had a duty beyond representing their clients' specific interests: to the court system itself. Most non-lawyers don't know that every day lawyers also wrestle with a multitude of commands contained in the professional rules by which they live. Some commands seem to conflict, principally the ones that require lawyers to advocate for their clients "zealously," but also "honestly." The concept of honesty is deliberately woven into what is an extremely adversarial trial system: lawyers fight hard, but while doing so, are required to be "candid" with the courts. They are forbidden to make misrepresentations, knowingly allow perjury, submit false evidence, or do any other dishonest or unethical thing in an attempt to strengthen their client's position. "Zeal" may only go so far. Any case may at any moment suddenly force a lawyer to decide how far to go in representing a current client without violating the ethical constraints of the system. "Candor" requires lawyers to disclose judicial precedent that bears upon their case, even if it hurts their client's cause. One of the most challenging situations arises when there is no precedent for the result the client seeks; how far can the lawyer go in presenting his case?

It is hard to answer that question without knowing something about how judges generally face a "no-precedent" situation. How do they "make law?" What principles do neutral judges follow?

Judge Richard Posner, a widely-respected former federal circuit judge, describes an "open area", in which a judge's vote "is determined not by some declared judicial philosophy and not by the orthodox materials of legal decision making." He agrees that judges are occasional "legislators," who, "like other people who have to make decisions under uncertainty, act in good faith but rely heavily on intuition, and also on emotion both as shaping intuition and as an independent influence of decision making."

Much earlier, Benjamin Cardozo, who served with great distinction on the New York Court of Appeals and the United States Supreme Court, said that the power of judges to declare the law "carries with it the power, and within limits the duty, to make law where none exists." He liked to quote the famed Yale Law School Professor Arthur Corbin, who had said that "it is the function of our courts to keep the [legal] doctrines up to date with the mores by continual restatement and by giving them a continual new content. This is judicial legislation, and the judge legislates at his peril. Nevertheless, it is the necessity and duty of such legislation that gives to judicial office its highest honor; and no brave and honest judge shirks the duty or fears the peril."

Cardozo believed that when "legislating" a judge has a "narrow range of choice," but "social justice" was the end to be attained. In his lectures published in 1921 under the title "The Nature of the Judicial Process," he said that "novel situations ... must be determined, as they arise, by considerations of analogy, of convenience, of fitness, and of justice." A judge walks a fine line because "the distinction between the subjective ... and the objective" is "shadowy and evanescent," So to Cardozo, the judicial process came down to "logic, and history, and custom, and utility, and the accepted standards of right conduct," which are "the forces which singly or in combination shape the progress of the law." Which of these forces dominates in any case "must depend largely upon the comparative importance or value of the social interests that will be thereby promoted or impaired."

He recognized that legal precedent was critically important, because it is a "fundamental social interest" that the law be "uniform and impartial. There must be nothing in its action that savors of prejudice or arbitrary whim or fitfulness. Therefore, in the main there shall be adherence to precedent." But there was a very big *caveat:*

> Uniformity ceases to be good when it becomes uniformity of oppression. The social interest served by symmetry or certainty must then be balanced against the social interest served by equity and fairness or other elements of social welfare … If you ask how [the judge] is to know when one interest outweighs another, I can only answer that he must get his knowledge just as the legislator gets it, from experience and study and reflection; in brief, from life itself.

The six cases in this book may help illustrate how both judges and lawyers navigate the imperatives in cases that fall into Posner's "open area," or where blindly following precedent would come close to "uniformity of oppression." In these cases, the lawyers and judges did make "new law," and in most of them, I believe that the judges intended to do "social justice."

From the Berg case, I learned early in my career the necessity (and the joy) of "making law," or trying to do so. Despite their unwillingness in that case to end the "no contribution" rule, the

RICHARD C. CAHN

judges seriously considered the possibility of doing so. Such a result may not please the client at the time, but the discussion that preceded it might yet, in the unseen future, hand a stunning victory to someone else's client who finds himself similarly situated.

A good tool aids lawyers' efforts to "make law:" Rule 3.1 of the American Bar Association's Model Rules of Professional Conduct allows lawyers to make "a good faith argument for an extension, modification or reversal of existing law." The rule is a bold invitation to creative thinking, but it also imposes a heavy obligation on a lawyer venturing down its path, as I did a few times.

So, this is about my unexpected and exciting adventures as an American trial lawyer, which began very early in my journey as an idealist and an optimist throughout an imperfect judicial system that embodies all the uncertainties of human judgment, but above all is solemnly charged with the duty to not only enforce the law, but also to do justice, no matter the identity or position of the parties.

Situations arise that do not fit into an established and comfortable rubric. Fairness and justice may require a new approach, and I'd like to list here four judges who either took that approach or gave it serious consideration—Algernon Butler, Chief Judge of the United States District Court for the Eastern District of North Carolina; Charles P. Sifton, U.S. District Judge for the Eastern District of New York; Stanley Fuld, Judge (and later Chief Judge) of the New York Court of Appeals; and Judith Kaye, also Chief Judge of the same court—I consider them "giants" in our long and distinguished legal tradition.

I don't want to give the impression that law only consists of great and widely-significant actions. Sometimes doing the right thing seems trivial and can be difficult; but it is usually right.

During the trial of the so-called "triple murder case" before hard-bitten Bronx Supreme Court Justice George Carney, Lenny

Wexler and I were having a conference in Carney's chambers when the judge erupted with surprisingly inflammatory remarks about the character and guilt of our client, over whose fate he was presiding. When we returned to the courtroom, we immediately placed the judge's prejudicial comments on the very public trial record. Carney could not believe what he was hearing, loudly banged his gavel, and ordered us back into his chambers. Once inside, he glared at us, and with a bright red face, shouted, "I thought things we say in chambers are off the record." We made it clear to him that we considered our duty to our client to take precedence over any duty of courtesy to him. To his credit, he let it go.

The aim of this book—other than to recount some wonderful events—is to show how important to our way of life it is to have both an independent judiciary and a fearless and principled Bar, where those working on both sides of the Bench are willing not only to speak truth to power, but to put a stop to its excesses when necessary.

4
THE ARMY BOTCHES COEDUCATION

It took 174 years from the founding of the United States Military Academy at West Point for coeducation to arrive, but less than one for the chain of command to sabotage it.

On a cold winter day in 1977, Second-Class Cadet Finn Collins* was contemplating his future, which promised to be a bright one. He was already halfway through what in an ordinary college would be called his junior year; in a mere 15 months he would complete his arduous but rewarding years of military training and academic studies and receive the commission he had long coveted, as a Second Lieutenant in the United States Army.

But that reverie was interrupted when he was advised that a charge under the Academy's Disciplinary Code had been filed against him for "escorting a female fourth-class cadet [Alicia Romano*] in Eisenhower Hall," a new, large recreational and performing arts center on campus. Collins had barely digested that unsettling news when, two days later, he was informed of the filing of an additional charge, that he had again violated the Code by "associating" with Romano, this time by allowing her to be present in his room. A third charge was yet to follow, of "showing gross lack of judgment by escorting and fraternizing" with the same female cadet.

That the Army would bring even one such charge would have been stunning; that it had brought three was unthinkable. After opening West Point's doors to female cadets, the Academy had decided to continue to ban "escorting", "associating", and "fraternizing" between the sexes—prohibitions that had long been embedded in the pre-co-ed Disciplinary Code. It made no sense under the Academy's new circumstances, yet the triply-reinforced message, logical or not, was both clear and deadly serious, and Collins was not its only intended recipient. All members of the Corps of Cadets were being sharply reminded that the advent of coeducation had not changed the Disciplinary rules.

Collins had just been plunged into a tangled web of legal proceedings that would apparently be governed by none of the rules of fairness and due process that universally prevailed in America outside of the service academies. A Commandant's Board, the designated disciplinary tribunal, quickly processed the first two charges, found Collins guilty, and punished him by "awarding" him 40 demerits and 50 "disciplinary tours." A month later, a second Board, with no concerns about either double jeopardy or double punishment, imposed 70 more demerits and 60 more disciplinary tours for the same act of "escorting."

"Disciplinary tours" were serious punishments. The guilty cadet was required to march at a quick pace while carrying a heavy rifle. They were considerably more serious for Collins, who had recently undergone hospitalization and major surgery at Walter Reed Army Hospital, leaving him in a body, neck and head cast for eight weeks.

Major Gordon Kimball, an orthopedist at West Point who had Collins under his care for nearly two years, was impressed by the young man's extraordinary grit and determination. "It has been quite evident to me," he wrote, that he is in pain "at most times," but "seldom complains .... He is reluctant to come to Sick

Call because of the loss of time involved and other obligations which he has.... In spite of his difficult medical problems, and in spite of the time and investment involved in being taken care of, he has maintained an excellent attitude about his medical conditions and has impressed me with the fact that he seems determined to remain at the Academy and become a commissioned officer. Many others with lesser problems would have given up long ago and sought an easier road elsewhere. I strongly recommend that he be retained at the Academy. I think that he will make an excellent army officer."

Collins had never complained, but it was easy to imagine the degree to which his ever-present pain would be aggravated by those punishments.

In just a few weeks, yet another notice came: the next day a "Conduct Review Committee" would meet to consider whether Collins should be separated from the Academy for excessive demerits. Given less than 24 hours to prepare his defense, he strongly protested, and was grudgingly given a six-day adjournment.

It was September before the Committee began to consider his punishment, and Captain James Boyd, a lawyer and officer in the Judge Advocate General's Corps, was assigned to defend him.

But "defend" had a loose definition at West Point. Boyd would be excluded from the hearing sessions. Inside the hearing room, Collins would be alone. Only the Committee would have its lawyer present to hear the testimony, ask questions, and make objections.

For all its vaunted efficiency, West Point couldn't get its act together for this case: after only one day of testimony, the Committee "terminated" the proceeding because of a "procedural error." Collins and his lawyer tried to learn what the "error" was, but no one would give them the information. The official response was to summon him to a new hearing six days later. It was hardly shaping up as a fair fight.

It was no surprise when the committee recommended that he be separated from the Academy for excessive demerits.

The official at the Military Academy responsible for the training of the cadets is the Commandant of Cadets, whom the rules required to be an Academy graduate "of impeccable character and bearing with a record of academic excellence and demonstrated accomplishment in the field." In that fall, the Commandant was Brigadier General John C. Bard. On November 2, Bard approved Collins's separation, but considering his outstanding reputation, it was jarring to learn that he had placed material into Collins's disciplinary file that destroyed the integrity of the entire proceeding.

Collins did not know it yet, but a separate set of Honor Code charges arising out of his "associating" with Cadet Romano had been secretly drawn up charging him with lying about the relationship with Cadet Romano. Bard had the Honor Code file in his possession and attached it to the Disciplinary file for the Secretary of the Army to see.

Tainting consideration of one set of charges by including another set of charges that had never been proven is a "no-no" in any proceeding subject to "due process." Bard's action effectively convicted Collins on the untried Honor charges.

Collins learned what Bard had done and objected, but Bard declined to retract his action, and no one would show him the honor charges. Whatever objections he and his attorney made fell on deaf ears.

On December 15, General Andrew Goodpaster, the Academy's Superintendent and highest-ranking officer, sent the entire, now contaminated file, to Clifford Alexander, Jr., the Secretary of the Army, almost certainly expecting it to be rubber-stamped.

Only Secretary Alexander now stood between Collins and his fate: to lose his degree and his commission and be ordered to active duty for three years as an enlisted soldier. Compelled service in separation cases was designed to compensate the Army for its thwarted expectation that the free education and training it had provided to the expelled cadet would produce a new Second Lieutenant at the end of four years.

It was now December, just five months before Collins's scheduled graduation and commissioning.

Boyd, Collins's JAG lawyer, was extremely concerned. He had been advising Collins on his legal rights to the best of his ability outside of the hearing room. But he did not like the way things were going.

The Judge Advocate General's Corps is made up of lawyers and commissioned officers, often intending to make the Army a permanent career. They can be assigned either to prosecute or defend those charged with Honor Code and Disciplinary Code violations.

Boyd confirmed what I had heard, that the military careers of JAG defense lawyers who win too many cases are sometimes negatively affected, although some of them are simply plucked out of their defense roles and reassigned to prosecution duty. It was a credit to JAG lawyers that most took seriously their duty as members of the Bar to defend someone, even though they knew that their efforts, particularly if successful, were almost certain to irritate a more important someone up in the chain of command who, long before, would likely have prejudged the case. Boyd was certainly willing to continue his defense efforts, but he was deeply worried about the probable outcome.

Another factor strongly influenced Boyd's thinking. When Collins's case arose, coeducation at West Point, after so many years of exclusively male officer training, was still new, and the public was intensely interested in knowing how it was working. Boyd believed that for reasons that were never clear, some of the Army brass had set out to make a public example of Collins by expelling him from the Academy, and details of the case would almost certainly become public. The pressures on the various administrative boards, upon him as JAG counsel, and upon Collins himself, would greatly increase. He thought that outside counsel, free of military career concerns, would be more effective in Collins's defense.

Accepting Boyd's guidance, Collins contacted former Congressman James Grover, who was practicing law in Collins's home town of Babylon, Long Island. Jim Grover had been my Congressman, and I knew him personally. He called me; I told him that I would be glad to take the case and met Collins in my office a week later.

So began my introduction to the strange world of military discipline. I had never seen copies of the West Point Honor Code or Disciplinary Rules and knew nothing about the rules governing proceedings under either set of rules. I called Bob Armstrong, a friend from the days he and I were young lawyers practicing in Huntington village. Bob had once been a JAG officer, and since those young years he had moved to Virginia, where he practiced military law, representing uniformed service members and occasionally midshipmen at Annapolis, several hours away. I could not have had a better teacher for my cram course in Disciplinary and Honor Code rules at the service academies; how they were interpreted and enforced, and how they related to each other.

The most important thing I did was listen to my new client and read his own handwritten account of what he had, and had not, done, and what impact the Army's proceedings had had on him.

His words were heartbreaking, and had the unmistakable ring of truth. We incorporated what he had written, verbatim, into an affidavit that he would sign, that we would soon place before a federal judge. Collins set out his unblemished record at the West Point, pointed out how slim the charges were ("walking with a female cadet, having her present in my room and being in a phone booth with her"), and continued…

> …at all times, my conduct towards her was that befitting a gentleman and officer of the United States Army. I was never charged nor did I ever engage in any illicit sexual activity despite the fact that my relationship with this cadet as it developed could be characterized as one of emotional attachment…. My association with her initially was for the purpose of aiding and counseling her relative to her contemplated resignation from the Academy.

Collins described the relationship "is only what one would naturally and normally expect to develop between a young man and woman," and then plaintively raised the obvious question: "I am at a loss to understand why I am being punished for becoming emotionally involved with a woman."

Just those two documents, Collins's own affidavit and the report from his orthopedist, were the most powerful legal papers that we submitted to the Court. One could not read them without concluding that it was unjustified, inappropriate and legally untenable for the Academy to have brought such charges.

I like to remember this case as the time when I—a decidedly non-military type—declared war on the U.S. Army, and it surrendered.

Our extraordinary campaign was soon to catch the attention of the news media, seemingly all over the Western Hemisphere. I cannot tell you how many calls from reporters we received.

The "we" I am referring to included David Neufeld, a recent graduate of Case Western Law School, a bright and idealistic

MAKING LAW

young lawyer who was associated with me in my practice and worked with me on the Collins case.

David and I both believed that law was a useful tool to remedy injustice, and that the most critical part of our presentation to the judge who would hear any case was the statement of facts. In this case, Collins's own narrative that had so moved me became the most poignant and persuasive part of that recital, and it cried out for a judge's intervention.

The case was in many ways a textbook example of injustice, multiple violations of due process, and command influence. It had all the legal defects that a defense lawyer can only dream of. Boyd soon provided more icing for the legal cake whose ingredients we were now combining: one of the Cadet officers had been openly telling members of Collins's company that "there hadn't been enough Honor Code convictions, and there ought to be more." When I heard that, I knew how the word "drumbeat" came to mean what it does.

Even with so much going for us, the case presented a major legal challenge, because the Courts had long made it clear that the Army has full authority to discipline cadets.

Judges defer to the military, correctly believing that Army officers know more about military discipline than they do. In wartime, no one outside of the military can ever be in a position to second-guess battle orders, and the same deference long ago had found its way into court cases involving a hapless cadet at West Point or a midshipman at the Naval Academy who had gotten into trouble and was being disciplined.

And yet, West Point is more than a military academy; it is also a public university, and I knew from my years as Regional Counsel at SUNY - Stony Brook that authorities in public universities who take disciplinary actions against students must comply with the U.S. Constitution. Courts look carefully at what government institutions do and will reverse an action that a public university has taken if it violates somebody's constitutional rights. And the U. S. Military Academy at West Point was a public university.

So, the question that a judge would have to answer was clear-cut: which legal principle was more important, that West Point was a public entity bound to extend to its students the protections afforded by the Constitution, or that it was an integral part of the U.S. military, whose decisions were necessarily given unquestioned deference by the courts?

In my view, the facts pushed the balance away from the deference side of the scale. Co-education had been instituted at West Point without the authorities having taken the necessary time and effort to reframe the institution's rules governing the relationships between the sexes on campus. What the Academy had done was just too intrusive and unreasonable; it had essentially criminalized innocent human activity. Before the Collins charges, it was highly unlikely that anyone among the new, co-ed Corps of Cadets would have assumed that they were prohibited from "associating" with a cadet of the opposite sex, or from talking or walking together.

However, the Army was employing its most heavy-handed tactics to enforce just such prohibitions, and however contrary to common sense the charges were, it was urgent to address them. They had been endorsed by the highest-ranking officials at West Point, and the clock was quickly running out.

It was difficult to read the legal documents and not conclude that the Army was punishing Collins, not for actions reasonably deemed detrimental to good order and discipline, but merely for his associations, which seemed a clear violation of the Constitution's First Amendment. Since there was no case law dealing with that situation, I thought there was virtually no chance that a judge would strike down the charges on that ground, but we included a First Amendment argument in our court papers, just in case.

MAKING LAW

We thought the claim that Collins wasn't given due process would probably appeal to a judge more, as it was supported by a number of court decisions and was therefore more clear-cut. Also, it was easily provable. The Academy had never given Collins a reasonable opportunity to assemble a defense in a case which, if lost, would immediately terminate the military career which he had long dreamed about, to which he had already devoted more than three years of his life.

We had to finish our papers before something irrevocable happened. As soon as we could draw them and have them signed by Collins, I would drive to Brooklyn to file the case and ask the judge who would be assigned to it to direct the Army to suspend all of the pending proceedings. The judge would need time to consider the whole case carefully before rendering a final decision, but in the meantime, we would try to pause the Army's unrelenting march toward Collins's expulsion. I worried about which judge would be assigned to the case, but that decision was out of my hands.

As we worked to finish the papers, something was changing behind the scenes. It was now January 1978, and the records that we had been unsuccessfully demanding for two months were suddenly delivered to us. And then, within days, Bland West, the Army's Deputy General Counsel, called from Washington to advise us that the Secretary of the Army had "returned" to the Military Academy Commandant Bard's recommendation that Collins be separated. The Pentagon's lawyers had decided that the Conduct Board was improperly constituted because it lacked a required lieutenant colonel member, and that Bard had committed prejudicial error by submitting the Honor Code materials to the Conduct Board. The failure to assign a lieutenant colonel was apparently the "procedural" error that no one would disclose several months before. But time was still against us. Graduation was now four months away.

Then the Honor Code file showed up at our office. The chain of command at West Point had been holding it in reserve, and the fact that Collins's association with another cadet had now been elevated to an "Honor" violation made it infinitely more dangerous than the original disciplinary charges.

West Point's ancient Honor Code flatly states, "A cadet shall not lie, cheat or steal, or tolerate those who do", an ethical as well as practical commandment that had been drummed into generations of cadets, and for good reason: truthfulness is absolutely required on the battlefield; it has also long been an ironclad expectation during the entire period of military education and training at the service academies. There are "no exceptions" to the truthfulness requirement. "Lying" is not limited to untruths; it also encompasses "quibbling," meaning failure to disclose the whole truth. That quaint English term is a specific Honor Code offense.

There was considerable discretion in the handling and punishment of disciplinary violations, but none when dealing with Honor Code charges. A single act of "quibbling" mandates a cadet's expulsion.

How carefully I reviewed those charges! I had not previously had a window into the efforts by the chain of command to escalate the matter in that way, and the only good thing that I could see in the file was that there had been several other proposed Honor Code charges in the early stages of the prosecution that were so outrageous that they had immediately been rejected by the legal officers at the Academy.

One was so subjective that no one could possibly determine its truth or falsity: it charged Collins with lying "by telling Major Boyd Harris in April 1977 that he did not love Alicia Romano." That was too much for Colonel Gerald W. Davis, who was Staff

MAKING LAW

Judge Advocate, the highest-ranking legal officer at West Point. As soon as he saw it, Davis recommended that the charge "be eliminated as it was nebulous, involved the uncertainty of emotion, the possibility of jest, and could otherwise be explained away without difficulty."

But, undeterred, the prosecution staff had drawn up a new set of five charges.

Procedural irregularities had begun to multiply. The prior November, the Honor Board at the center of this separate whirlwind of activity, had returned all five recommendations to the Commandant because Cadet Collins had not been informed of three of the new charges until after the first Subcommittee met. The Honor Board then directed that if the matter were to be presented to another subcommittee, it should be composed of new members.

Doggedly, the prosecutors formed a new subcommittee, and within a week it referred the new charges to a Full Honor Board. The new claims stretched back more than a year: one accused Collins of "lying" and "quibbling," by telling two fellow cadets that his Battalion Executive Officer, Cadet James Renfrow, Jr., had authorized him to fraternize with Cadet Romano. Renfrow had graduated from West Point a year before and was now on active duty elsewhere as a Second Lieutenant. He was a key missing witness, and he was never called to testify; my opinion was that it was highly unlikely that he would ever have been ordered to leave his current duties to return to West Point to testify against a cadet in a case that did not involve the commission of a serious crime.

Less than three weeks after the new Honor Board referral, Bard again recommended that the Army Secretary separate Collins.

However, Colonel Davis was now unhappy with the five new Honor charges, and in January, they were revised and sent to the

Commandant, who sent them to a Full Honor Board on the same day. That "Full" board hearing was scheduled for February 28.

Faced with official activity now taking place on multiple fronts, we had to finish up our legal papers. We completed what by now had become a very long complaint, charging some 13 procedural violations and detailing each infringement upon Collins's constitutional rights. The Army's punishment of Cadet Collins had been cruel and inhuman, given his medical infirmities and the commencement of numerous and repetitive proceedings against him. The letter from Major Kimball, the orthopedist, attesting to Collins's courage and determination, and Collins's own words gave the Court more than a glimpse into the human being at the heart of the case.

We filed the case in late February, naming Secretary of the Army Clifford Alexander as a defendant. It was immediately assigned to Judge Charles P. Sifton, known to his friends as "Tony," a tall, thin man, whom I was told was a quintessential intellectual, and who, with a distinguished white beard, looked the part.

Sifton was appointed by President Jimmy Carter and had only been on the bench for four months; I had not yet met him. Had I known then that he would soon develop a reputation for fairness as well as toughness, I would have felt that his selection by the random assignment system was a stroke of good fortune. All I knew about him was that he had been an Assistant U.S. Attorney and later a partner in a large Manhattan law firm, and that he had been married to the daughter of the theologian Reinhold Niebuhr. He was considered to be very smart, and I hoped for the best.

Even cautious optimism on the part of a trial lawyer is sometimes just bravado, and I didn't feel brave. What was about to occur would either rescue Cadet Collins's military career or utterly fail. And many future classes of cadets would also be affected by the result in this case. West Point's "fraternization" rules would either change—or they would not.

I was tense as I entered Sifton's chambers late in the afternoon of February 24. Assistant U.S. Attorney Robert Begleiter, from the U.S. Attorney's office in Brooklyn, was present to represent the Army. He and I began to state our positions.

Sifton had not had much time to read our papers before he invited us in, but he had mastered the critical facts and repeatedly interrupted each of us with pointed questions. We finished up in about a half an hour. For a few moments, no one spoke, and I wondered whether I should have said more.

Thirty minutes was a pretty short period of time to decide the future of someone's life. But that was all the time Sifton needed.

He did not ask us to excuse ourselves, as judges often do, while he retired to discuss the matter with his law clerks. "Gentlemen," he began, and then he paused, with either intended or unintended dramatic effect, and said: "I'm going to issue a TRO here," he said. "TRO" stood for a temporary restraining order, which he began to write out by hand, staying the United States Army from proceeding with the Honor Board proceedings against Cadet Collins pending further order of the Court.

Collins would be "immediately and irreparably injured", he wrote,

> by being proceeded against before the full Honor Board on the scheduled date since his private life and friendships and his honor will be questioned before his peers at the Academy and his character and reputation affected by the examination which will then take place.

To my surprise, Sifton had seized upon our last-minute First Amendment argument: the Army had no right to interfere with

Collins's personal relationships. Then he wrote another paragraph, specifically questioning,

> whether plaintiff has been afforded due process ... and whether there is a constitutional basis for the proceedings being conducted against plaintiff.

That went even beyond what we dreamed a judge would do. Sifton was not only going to compel West Point, military institution or not, to afford this cadet due process while conducting legal proceedings against him; he was at least flirting with the idea that the Academy may not have had a constitutional right to bring these proceedings at all.

To all appearances Sifton never considered taking the traditional path, by deferring to the decisions taken by the military and denying us a stay. What clearly outweighed that line of precedent was that he believed that on at least two grounds, West Point had violated Collins's constitutional rights, a conviction that had to have been instinctive on Sifton's part, since he had hardly had time to do very much legal research on the case.

Our attack on West Point then hit the press, and "firestorm" was a pretty good description of what it was like. David and I could not have hoped for a better reaction. Skeptical reporters were on our side, making clear to us, and in the stories they wrote, their negative view of the Army's decision to charge Cadet Collins; they performed their First Amendment role as skeptics with brash aplomb. They asked us why we thought the Army was taking such a hard line (we couldn't speculate on that), and also what happened to Cadet Romano (we did not know that either, and only learned later that, sadly, she had resigned from the Academy).

We began to receive telephone calls seeking comment from newspaper and radio reporters all over North America. A few days after Judge Sifton signed the TRO, I picked up the telephone to find a reporter from a radio station in Puerto Rico on the line.

Paul Rigby, the sardonic and prize-winning cartoonist for the *New York Post*, drew a wonderful cartoon showing two cadet officers decked out in their dress uniforms with tall feathered dress hats and white gloves, stuffing a hapless cadet into the mouth of a cannon with a long pole. The caption read, "Here at West Point, we have ways of punishing cadets who have women in their rooms!" The original of that cartoon hangs on the wall in my home, and I laugh every time I see it.

The Army never did put in any opposing papers. Begleiter called me to adjourn the court proceedings; he was having continual conferences with his clients, and went to the Pentagon to discuss the case with the Army's top brass in person; the Army would not contest Judge Sifton's restraining order, and no action would be taken against Collins in the meantime. Begleiter made no other promises. He was businesslike but seemed sympathetic to our cause.

On March 9, two weeks after we had appeared before Sifton, Begleiter called again, and I was now speaking to a much more relaxed, and apparently relieved, adversary. The Army was withdrawing all disciplinary and Honor Code charges. Our client would be free to take his final exams, graduate and be commissioned. Which he did.

I wondered whether Collins's problem at West Point would follow him throughout his military career, but it apparently did not. He rose to the rank of Captain and retired to civilian life, and as of 2017 was still listed in the Military Academy's directory of living alumni.

A quarter of a century after these events, Begleiter, with whom I was then serving on the federal court's magistrate judge screening committee, told me that the fact that Collins was a talented pitcher on West Point's varsity baseball team was a big factor in resolving the case. When Begleiter went to discuss the litigation with the Pentagon, he had told me that "people from West Point" accompanied him. I had assumed that he was referring to the JAG prosecutors. But now he told me that the most important person traveling with him to Washington was the West Point baseball coach, whose recital of Collins's exploits on the baseball diamond resonated with the Pentagon brass.

"Right!" I thought.

My second thought was, Well, maybe there was something in his explanation; but could there possibly have been a few other factors at work as well?

Although Begleiter never told me what he discussed with his clients (other than Collins's baseball prowess), I got the distinct impression that he had worked behind the scenes to persuade the Pentagon that the Army's case had been misconceived and poorly handled, and should be discontinued. Part of what went into my assumption was that there was too much wrong with what the Army did for a good lawyer not to notice. I have always admired lawyers like Begleiter who do the right thing when their clients haven't, and who recognize that their integrity, and that of their office (the U.S. Attorney's office for the Eastern District of New York in Begleiter's case), rides on each decision they make.

This experience reminded me of memories from my earliest days as a practicing lawyer. There was an assistant district attorney named Henry Devine who for many years handled appeals for the Nassau County District Attorney's office. He was a legend admired by young and old members of the local bar and by the judges for his integrity and candor. I was present on one of the many occasions when he stood in the appeals court in Brooklyn to confess to the judges that a criminal conviction his colleagues in the DA's office had toiled to obtain was flawed and should be set

MAKING LAW

aside. Lawyers like Begleiter and Devine are priceless assets of the legal system.

And so was Judge Sifton, who gave the Army a chance to catch its breath and reflect, not merely upon baseball, but also upon its failure to modify its regulations to account for the many interactions between male and female cadets that would be inevitable so long as West Point remained a co-ed campus.

I originally wondered if the Army had done so; perhaps there was a memo somewhere in West Point's files about "lessons learned" in our case. I was hoping that Sifton's pointed reminder about cadets' private lives and honor, and perhaps the media coverage including Rigby's trenchant cartoon, would encourage the Army to find the proper balance between maintaining discipline and protecting the rights of its Cadets—of both sexes.

But battles remain to be fought in the service academies, and present-day cases do not reflect the concerns that Judge Sifton voiced. The pendulum has swung away from the protection of individual cadets. As recently as 2017, the Court of Appeals for the Second Circuit dismissed a case, Doe v. Hagenbeck, brought by a female former West Point cadet, who claimed that she was raped on campus by a male cadet, and that the Superintendent and Commandant of Cadets at the Academy had created a "policy that discriminated against female cadets, tolerated attacks against [them] and discouraged reporting," and "promoted a sexually aggressive culture." If her allegations are true, the Court said, "they are no credit to West Point." But, echoing a Supreme Court decision that was issued five years after Judge Sifton acted in our case, the judges ruled that Cadet Doe's claim could not proceed, because of "the inescapable demands of military discipline [that] cannot be taught on the battlefield." The Court ruled that it would be "inappropriate" for the judges to create a remedy for enlisted military personnel against their superior officers.

Although there are legal differences between the 2017 case and Collins's—and some may question whether the critical difference is that Collins was a male cadet and Doe was a female cadet—it is clear that the tide is running in a different direction than it was in the 1970s. One judge on the appeals panel, Denny Chen, strongly disagreed with his two colleagues, saying that Doe's injuries did not arise "incident to military service" at all:

> When she was subjected to a pattern of discrimination, and when she was raped, ... she was simply a student, and her injuries were incident only to her status as a student.... The actions and decisions she now challenges had nothing to do with military discipline and command.

Collins and Doe played out in dramatically different ways; the path taken can depend entirely upon which judges get to choose. As seen by the 2-1 decision in the Doe case, even judges in the same case can disagree on the appropriate result.

The principal conclusion to be drawn from these cases (as well as the continuing legislative and administrative proceedings in the Baby Jane Doe matter which are described in the following chapter) is that some legal battles seem destined to be fought again and again, unless some existing legal authority has definitively settled the issue. Yet "definitively" is more easily said than done: in the Doe case, even a 1983 Supreme Court decision that supposedly settled the issue only convinced two of the three appeal judges that the rape victim could not sue. Each time the issue is relitigated, people may see it differently and the result changes.

My take on this is, that if enough people consider an issue important, and its resolution at a particular moment in time, whether by Congress, state legislatures, or by the courts, fails to command wide support in the national community—and sometimes, even if it does—groups or factions particularly interested in it will challenge it again, usually in the courts, where the judges will have a special duty to explain and justify their reasons for reaching a particular result. Over time, by the accumulation of successive court decisions involving a variety of fact patterns, a more durable consensus may emerge and the issue laid to rest for that moment in history, but not necessarily permanently, because at a future date, people may again question what the courts or the legislatures have done. *Stare decisis*, the legal doctrine that theoretically requires us all to "stand by things decided," has a finite duration. It, like history itself, is always open to question.

5

WHO WILL TAKE CARE OF BABY JANE DOE?

By October 15, 1983, I had been serving as State University's Regional Counsel for 11 years, performing a variety of legal tasks, mostly at the Stony Brook campus, one of New York's four "University Centers" for research and teaching.

On that lazy Saturday afternoon, I answered our home phone and heard the flat Midwestern voice of Carl Hanes, the University's Vice President for Finance and Management.

Carl was my principal contact at Stony Brook. When there was a situation on campus that needed legal attention, he would call, and inform me in his low-key, matter of fact way, usually with a touch of irony in his voice, what needed my attention. Carl was one of my favorite Stony Brook people.

On that Saturday in October, however, the agitation in his voice was obvious. A state trial-level judge, Frank DeLuca, had just appeared at University Hospital on the Stony Brook campus, accompanied by two men: Mark Cohen, the Chief Assistant District Attorney in Suffolk County, and a man named A. Lawrence Washburn (Carl did not know who he was). DeLuca told a startled receptionist and the hospital's administrators, that he was there "to hold a hearing" on the medical condition of a newborn baby girl

MAKING LAW

in the hospital's neonatal intensive care unit. He wanted to see the doctors on the case. Immediately.

The administrators ushered the judge into a small conference room and paged the doctors. Then they called Carl, who immediately called me. Thus, I began my brief cameo appearance in a new and jarring campus drama.

The baby, soon to become known as "Baby Jane Doe," had been born at nearby St. Charles Hospital in Port Jefferson. At birth, she suffered from severe medical problems, including spina bifida (the bones and tissues of the baby's spinal cord had failed to fully close); microcephaly (an unusually small head usually accompanied by abnormal brain development); and hydrocephalus(excess fluid in the cranial cavity leading to damaging pressure on the brain). St. Charles was not equipped to perform surgery, and the baby had been transferred to Stony Brook.

At Stony Brook Hospital, physicians evaluated her condition, and advised her parents of the available medical options: a shunt could be placed to relieve the pressure of fluid pressing on the brain, and the opening in the spine could be surgically closed to lessen the likelihood of infection. However, surgery carried the risk of almost certain loss of what little function remained in the baby's legs. An alternative course of treatment would be simply to administer antibiotics and to make sure that she was kept hydrated and comfortable.

Neither choice would place the infant in imminent risk of death and both were within the accepted standards of medical treatment. With great anguish, the parents declined the surgery.

DeLuca told the hospital personnel that he would decide whether he agreed with that decision. If he did not, he would order custody of the baby to be taken away from her parents so that surgery could be performed despite their objections.

The University and the parents were blindsided; no one had known the judge was coming, or that any questions had been raised by anyone about the child's care.

Carl and I finished our conversation. I called the hospital and asked to speak to DeLuca. Something didn't sound right, and I wanted to ask him directly what his intentions were. Legally, he had no authority to act until papers had been served upon at least one defendant, and neither the parents nor the University had received anything at all. That was not a trivial detail: unless DeLuca knew something we did not know, he had no business being at the hospital that day at all.

The judge came on the line. He told me that he had received a complaint from Mr. Washburn that the newborn girl was not being given appropriate medical care. Washburn wanted DeLuca to order the baby released to his custody for "proper care."

I asked DeLuca what Mr. Washburn's relationship was to the child. "He's not related at all," he said. Washburn was a Vermont resident who felt that the hospital, the parents and the doctors were "letting this baby die."

"A Vermont resident?" I repeated, and elaborated my question: "A stranger from another state has travelled to New York to sue this baby's parents because he was dissatisfied with a decision that someone told him a mother and father made about the medical care to be provided to their child?" The answer was yes.

I later learned Washburn was originally a municipal bond attorney in New York City, a field not ordinarily associated with medical disputes. He had become active in the national "Right to Life" movement and at some point moved to Vermont to start his own law practice.

Probably some hospital employee, angered by the parents' decision, had alerted the Right to Life group, and this sudden invasion of University Hospital was the result of that "tip."

Having answered my questions, DeLuca turned to the business that he had come to perform. He now bluntly asked me, "Are you going to represent the hospital in this matter or not? If so, please get over here. I'll wait to start until you arrive."

At this point, I still assumed that the judge had the necessary legal papers that Washburn, or someone acting in his behalf, had prepared, and if I went to the hospital, I would be served with them. But that would have placed me and the University in an impossible position. I would have been forced to go into a hearing blind, without seeing the files and without any opportunity to review the medical records or interview the doctors and the parents. For another reason, this was a serious legal situation, counselling caution: the presence of a representative from the D.A.'s office had injected criminal overtones into the conversation. But in this case, I had a better reason not to travel to Stony Brook: I had no authority to comply with the judge's request. "Judge," I told him, "the legal defense of the University in a litigation is the duty of the Attorney General, not mine."

"Well, who should be served with the papers?"

"I'll find out and advise you, judge, but in the meantime, would you please leave the hospital?"

There was silence. DeLuca appeared to be weighing his options; there was a very long pause. He finally seemed to realize that he was on thin ice. "OK, Dick," he said, "I'll leave at this time. But," he reminded me, "I want to hold this hearing as quickly as possible."

I immediately called Sanford Levine, the University's counsel, at his home in Niskayuna, NY, a small suburb outside of Albany. I had come to know Sandy a couple of years after the 1968 "drug bust" at Stony Brook, which I had investigated at the request of the University's Chancellor. Sandy was then a Deputy in SUNY Counsel's office. He was a gentle, unassuming man, and in all the years I knew him, even after he himself became General Counsel for the entire SUNY system, I never saw his ego get the better of his common sense.

At least once a year he loved to have the University's regional counsels from around the state—there were four of us—come to Albany to exchange ideas with him and each other. We would sit around his desk and discuss whatever difficult or unusual legal issues different campuses of the University system were then grappling with, and then Sandy would lead us next door to the Hudson River Club, which was located in Albany's abandoned and later refurbished railroad station.

Sandy was a member of that club, and he had extracted an important price for his membership. Several members, who like Sandy were prominent men in Albany, had invited him to join, but he had refused because the club would not accept women as members. Eventually he agreed to join, but only if his friends would vote with him to open up the club's membership to women. They agreed, and not long after Sandy joined, women began to be regularly seen at its dining tables, not as guests, but finally as members.

Sandy, like Carl Hanes, was not usually given to hyperbole, but he could get angry when someone did something that offended his sense of decency. This was one of those occasions; a measured, matter-of-fact, and logical analysis of this situation was inadequate.

He was furious. The sudden invasion of the University's hospital by the Judge and his strange entourage was unprecedented. But, characteristically, Sandy's emotions quickly abated, and gave way to working through our options. It was clear that it would be better for the University to know sooner rather than later what it was being accused of. So, he authorized me to accept service of the legal papers for the University.

They were delivered to me two days later, on Monday. When I looked at them, I was even more incredulous about what had happened. The lawsuit was not signed and dated until the day before, Sunday, October 16; contrary to what DeLuca had led me to believe, no lawsuit was in existence on Saturday when he and his companions were at the hospital. I had never had that kind of an experience with a judge before.

Washburn's involvement came from his affiliation with the "Right to Life Committee," which, I gathered, felt it had a roving and perpetual assignment to preserve life. It seemed that if it came to the group's attention that health care providers or even parents of a child anywhere in the country were standing in the way of what *they* believed was "appropriate medical treatment," the Committee, or one of its members, would try to intervene legally and change the outcome.

I digested this. Putting to one side the ethics of the situation—how could a group that is a stranger to a private family think it could make its medical decisions—I could not think of a way such a group would be able legally to obtain a copy of confidential medical records, or otherwise be in a position to form an opinion as to what medical care would or would not be appropriate.

Out of ignorance or intensity, it appeared that Washburn had gone to see Judge DeLuca at his Commack chambers that Saturday morning, without signed legal papers of any kind with him. The Judge reacted immediately to Washburn's narrative, made a decision to go to the hospital, and called the District Attorney's office to ask them to send someone to accompany him. For some reason, the Judge was not inhibited by the absence of legal papers. I wondered whether the D.A.'s office had thought to ask for them before agreeing to send a representative to the hospital.

On Sunday, the papers were prepared and signed, and Washburn brought them to DeLuca, who signed an Order directing the State to show cause why he should not name a "guardian" for Baby Jane to be empowered to direct the hospital to perform surgery. When I received the papers at my house on Monday,

RICHARD C. CAHN

David Smith, an Assistant State Attorney General stationed on Long Island, prepared to appear on behalf of the Hospital.

By Tuesday morning, the County Attorney's office had been informed of these events and entered the case. Lewis Silverman, a young Assistant County Attorney who was handling cases for the County's child abuse office, reviewed the law that appeared to govern the case, the New York "Family Court Act."

Silverman is a jolly man with a twinkle in his eyes, warm and friendly, and with his white mustache and beard, he looks a bit like an aging hippie. He was always a careful lawyer, priding himself on his ability to put aside personal emotions and concentrate instead upon what the law actually said before he decided what legal position he would take in a dispute. When I talked with him many years after the 1983 events, he was the director of the legal aid clinic at Touro Law School, teaching law students how to represent clients who lacked the funds to retain their own lawyers.

DeLuca had signed his order on Sunday, but when the papers were physically filed with the Court the next day, the new case was not assigned to him but instead to Melvyn Tanenbaum, a balding, severe, no-nonsense local judge. As it happens, both judges were from my hometown and I had known them both for some time before either became a Supreme Court justice. Tanenbaum was as doubtful about Washburn's standing as I had been, and named William Weber, a local attorney, to be the child's guardian. Despite no longer being officially a party to the case, Washburn, whom Silverman remembered as a "tall, angular, Ichabod Crane sort of fellow," hung around to see what would happen.

On Tuesday afternoon, October 18, Tanenbaum began a hearing at his courtroom in Riverhead. Silverman had interviewed the physicians and assured himself that the requirements of the Family Court Act had been strictly followed. The parents had been advised of all reasonable medical options and given the opportunity to choose among them, and the law seemed clear: only the parents had the right to decide which of the accepted medical approaches would be followed in their child's case. The parents had exercised that right, and Silverman believed that this disposed of the entire matter. He pressed the point with Tanenbaum, whom he found totally unsympathetic.

Silverman could see that Assistant D.A. Cohen also strongly disagreed with his arguments; his impression was that both men thought that the parents were about to "commit a murder." Weber, the newly appointed guardian, had initially thought the court should order surgery, but once he reviewed the medical records, he wasn't so sure.

Silverman himself, meanwhile, was facing unexpected opposition from the county's Child Protective Services agency, which originally wanted to side with Washburn. Silverman laid out the law books and was able to persuade the agency's decision-makers that no criminal charge of any kind can arise under New York law where parents have chosen one of the acceptable medical options for their child.

Even the CPS support of the parents left Tanenbaum unmoved; but late Wednesday, he realized that even with surgery the baby would have an increased risk of infection, pneumonia and epilepsy, and ordered that it should be performed on her, not immediately but as soon as "medically advisable." The vital point he made was that Baby Jane Doe "has an independent right to survive, and that right must be protected by the State." The parents were stunned.

Earlier, Smith and Silverman had alerted the Appellate Division, the appeals court, that its judges might be needed to intervene in the case. The judges were standing by prepared to immediately stay any order by Tanenbaum; and so they did, directing the lawyers to appear in Brooklyn to argue the case before them the next day.

The arguments concluded in mid-afternoon on Thursday, and the judges ordered the lawyers to stand by for a decision. The lights in the Brooklyn courthouse on Monroe Street remained on into the evening, as the lawyers spread out in the Court's lounge waiting. Hours later, just before midnight, printed copies of the judges' decision were distributed by the Clerk.

In blunt language, the appeals court unanimously overruled Tanenbaum. There was no evidence, they said, that the child's parents had been neglectful of their child:

> These concededly concerned and loving parents have made an informed, intelligent and reasonable determination based upon and supported by responsible medical authority. We find the parents' determination to be in the best interest of the infant. Accordingly, there is no basis for judicial intervention.

Cohen read the decision and immediately called his boss, District Attorney Patrick Henry (yes, that was his name!), to give him the news. They immediately decided to withdraw from the case, and did, thus ending the D.A.'s support for the Right to Life effort to remove the baby from her parents' custody.

However, Weber, the newly-appointed "guardian," who had earlier begun to doubt his position, decided to press ahead with the case. The next morning, he filed the necessary papers for an immediate appeal to the Court of Appeals.

The high court also broke speed records in hearing the matter and issuing its decision condemning "the unusual, and sometimes offensive" activities of "those who sought to displace parental responsibility" (meaning Washburn and Weber), and found that Judges DeLuca and Tanenbaum had had "no justification" to entertain the case:

> The Supreme Court initiated the proceeding at the behest of a person who had no disclosed relationship with the child, her parents, her family, or those treating her illnesses. Indeed, it does not appear that the petitioner had any direct or personal knowledge of the facts relating to the child's condition, the treatment she is presently receiving or the factors which prompted her parents to adopt the course they have. There is also no showing that the petitioner communicated his concerns to the Department of Social Services having primary responsibility with these matters ... The hearing court abused its discretion by permitting this proceeding to go forward.

Weber had pressed his argument that, as guardian, he had every right to pursue the case. The Court of Appeals judges responded firmly, and did not try to conceal their feelings:

> To accept the position of the guardian would have far-reaching implications ... Acceptance of the proposition he espouses would be to recognize the right of any person, without recourse to the strictures of the Family Court Act, to institute judicial proceedings which would catapult him into the very heart of a family circle, there to challenge the most private and most precious responsibility vested in the parents for the care and nurture of their

children—and at the very least to force the parents to incur the not inconsiderable expenses of extended litigation.

There are overtones to this proceeding which we find distressing. Confronted with the anguish of the birth of a child with severe physical disorders, these parents, in consequence of judicial procedures for which there is no precedent or authority, have been subjected in the last two weeks to litigation through all three levels of our State's court system. We find no justification for resort to or entertainment of these proceedings.

Unfortunately, that decision did not end the dispute. Ronald Reagan had become President two years before, and now the Right to Life movement enlisted the assistance of the federal government, which was glad to help. Just before the Court of Appeals decision, Reagan's Department of Health and Human Services demanded that University Hospital release Baby Jane Doe's medical records, so that HHS could determine whether Stony Brook was discriminating against a handicapped child by "withholding medically indicated treatment" from her.

Sandy Levine, again in a blistering mood, called HHS, bluntly gave them his views, and then followed up with a letter challenging the government's right to act. At this point he did not bother to conceal his abhorrence of what the government was trying to do. He was particularly outraged that, after full litigation of the issues in New York's courts, HHS would not let the matter rest.

Underlining HHS' offensive behavior, the agency had telephoned its request to University Hospital on a Friday night demanding access to the hospital at 10 a.m. the next day, but refused to put the request in writing or file a formal written complaint that the agency would have to defend in court.

That very year, a judge in the District of Columbia had struck down a regulation authorizing the government to intervene in such cases, saying there was serious doubt that the government under any circumstances had the right to involve itself in the treatment of newborns.

On November 2, the government filed a new case in the federal court on Long Island to compel University Hospital to surrender the records. A slew of "friends of the court" briefs opposing the government were prepared and filed before the case ended 15 days later: Baby Jane's parents, the American Hospital Association, the Hospital Association of New York, the American Medical Association, the American Civil Liberties Union, and the American Academy of Pediatrics all filed papers in support of the hospital.

The government's case was assigned to Leonard Wexler, who was sitting as a federal judge in a temporary court facility in an office building in Hauppauge, Long Island. The impressive Richard Meier-designed federal courthouse to be built in nearby Central Islip was still 14 years away. Wexler quickly dismissed the government's arguments, ruling that the papers submitted "conclusively demonstrate that the parents of Baby Jane Doe made a reasonable choice among possible medical treatments, acting with the best interests of the child in mind." Thus, he ruled, there was no basis for HHS to suspect a violation of the antidiscrimination law, and no justification for access to the baby's medical records.

That case ended four months later when the U. S. Court of Appeals in the Second Circuit agreed that the government had no right to interfere in medical decision-making with regard to newborn infants. The government decided not to take the case to the Supreme Court.

But, astonishingly, the dispute still did not end. On January 1984, Washburn filed a *third* case in the matter, in the federal court in Albany, seeking again to intervene in the medical situation as Baby Jane Doe's "next friend." District Judge Roger Miner, who was assigned to the case, was furious. Directly addressing Washburn, he gave him a large piece of his mind:

> THE COURT: The parents, having taken a position which they deem in the best interest of the child, which the courts have approved, and which you have been told through three decisions that have been made and now you come here and say, well now, you have got a constitutional right of some kind and because you have got a good reason to intervene in the affairs of this family, which the Court of Appeals told you to avoid doing –
>
> MR. WASHBURN: Your Honor, we deal here with a federal constitutional right.
>
> THE COURT: I know exactly what we deal with here, Mr. Washburn ... You can tell me why I should intervene in the affairs of this family by appointing an outside guardian for this child, and what the adverse interest is. What is the adverse interest you tell me about?
>
> Mr. WASHBURN: Because it deals with the voluntary acceptance of an untimely death. For the parents to make that decision for their child –
>
> THE COURT: Has someone told you somehow that they voluntarily accept the untimely death of their child? Are you privy to that somehow?

MAKING LAW

>MR. WASHBURN: Yes, and I have said so in the complaint.
>
>THE COURT: Say so in the complaint, and you say you are privy to that from them? Have you been told that? After hearing the arguments, I find and determine the plaintiff Washburn is barred from relitigating on her behalf. The New York Courts and the Eastern District have all found that Baby Jane's parents have been acting in their child's best interests. The claims asserted in this action have already been expressly repudiated. The Plaintiff has no standing to proceed even as a next friend. I find and determine that sanctions are warranted here. I dismiss all of the actions and provide sanctions in the sum of $500 to be paid by the plaintiff to the defendant.

Even that strong exchange, and the Court's rare imposition of a monetary fine on Washburn, failed to deter the Right to Lifers. At their behest, HHS promulgated a new set of regulations, giving itself the authority to intervene in cases like Baby Jane's. The American Medical Association and American Hospital Association sued the government, challenging the new regulations, and when the case reached the Supreme Court, the Justices invalidated them, finding that federal law did not authorize the government to give "unsolicited advice either to parents, to hospitals, or to state officials who are faced with difficult treatment decisions concerning handicapped children."

The case was an emotional experience for everyone involved. I never met the parents of Baby Jane Doe but had no doubt of their love for their child and their anguish. I also knew from my prior years of representing University Hospital, a teaching hospital, that its physicians, whose acts were also being called into question, were highly skilled and knowledgeable in their fields, and there was no reason to doubt their dedication to their patients' welfare. My telephone encounter with Judge DeLuca demonstrated total disregard of accepted court procedures and was personally offensive to me. My first reaction to hearing that a Vermont lawyer, a total stranger to the family, had taken it upon himself to "remedy" the situation, had been to think, "Who the hell does he think he is?"

In this case, the lawyers on both sides had quickly mobilized to fight what everyone saw as an exceptionally important battle, with issues going far beyond the fate of Baby Jane Doe.

Within a span of two weeks, a total of 14 judges had to choose between clashing social values, with no precedent to bind them. Two trial judges believed that they had to intervene to protect a defenseless newborn. In the abstract, that was not a bad motive. The first judge, DeLuca, felt so strongly about the subject that he was willing to show up at University Hospital and attempt to conduct an unprecedented, if not illegal, hearing by bullying the targets of his "judicial investigation" into immediately giving testimony under oath with no preparation or opportunity to consult with counsel.

None of the 12 judges in the appeal courts discerned any evidence of a murder plot in the case, but saw the facts as crying out for protection of the privacy and sanctity of a family and its exclusive right to make an agonizing decision that no family would ever want to make but that was thrust upon this one.

That decision was a policy choice mandated by no previous court decision. Different panels of judges might have made a different choice, and in a future case might, as the issues later continued to be hotly contested. When the federal government had weighed in, Surgeon General C. Everett Koop endorsed outside intervention in family medical decisions under some circumstances, emphasizing that "the life of a baby born with congenital birth defects should be protected, especially when there were contradictory medical diagnoses." Several years after that, to my surprise, President Clinton signed a bill into law amending the Child Abuse Prevention and Treatment Act (CAPTA), to make it easier for child welfare officials to intervene in such cases.

Baby Jane Doe survived. The spina bifida closed up by itself, a shunt was eventually installed, and *Newsday ran* an article in 2013 entitled "Baby Jane Doe at 30: Happy, Joking, Learning," with a photograph of an attractive and smiling young woman. She was in a wheelchair, was taking medication for seizures, and was wearing a body brace, but was learning how to live an independent life: every weekday she attended academic and physical therapy classes, away from home, and Friday night she returned to be with her parents. The family allowed use of her real first name, Keri-Lynn.

Someone will be fighting another Baby Jane Doe case sometime, in a continuing Sisyphean endeavor long into the future. Whoever it is will undoubtedly argue that the CAPTA amendment violates the parents' and the affected child's constitutional rights. I hope there will be a Sandy Levine and a Lewis Silverman available then, to keep that particular rock uphill where it belongs.

6
TILTING AT WINDMILLS

Spring 1962. The home phone rings. I look at the clock. It is 11 p.m. The caller had to be Fred. Another legal discussion is about to begin.

I did not know that this conversation would lead to my standing five years later before the Supreme Court in a case that produced national headlines, asking Chief Justice Earl Warren and his colleagues to completely revise the structure of our county government, which had remained virtually unchanged since it was created 279 years before, in 1683.

Fred Block and I were restless young lawyers trying to build our respective law practices, each hoping that some extraordinary legal challenge would arrive on our doorsteps once in a while. My father, who was my law partner, had been sidelined by a major heart attack, and my primary resource for sharing legal ideas was now Fred; apparently, I was his. His favorite time to call was a standing joke in my home.

This time, Fred had certainly come up with an exciting idea: he wanted to talk about a decision of the Supreme Court, a case called Baker v. Carr, that had been decided barely a week or so before.

Charles Baker, the Mayor of a Tennessee city, had challenged the method the State used when it divided itself into legislative

MAKING LAW

districts, and each of those districts elected one representative to represent it.

Tennessee was certainly not alone: every state legislature since the American Revolution really represented geographical areas, not people. Americans knew that cities and rural areas ordinarily had divergent and conflicting interests, so that citizens within a specific geographic area shared common values and concerns with one another that they did not necessarily share with those living elsewhere. Officials drawing maps of legislative districts tried to keep people sharing the same interests together.

The problem was that this procedure resulted in districts varying greatly in population.

Baker believed that kind of system was unfair to Tennessee's numerous urban residents who were usually packed together in small areas, in contrast to residents of sparsely-populated rural areas, who had a lot of open space between their homes. By the late 1950s, a city legislative district in Tennessee typically had many more residents than a rural legislative district, yet its population didn't matter; each district in the state had but a single legislator who was entitled to only that one vote. It was fair to say that on election day the vote of a citizen living in an urban district was worth a lot less than the vote of his counterpart living out in the countryside. That city dweller's voice in state government was "diluted."

The Equal Protection Clause in the Constitution's Fourteenth Amendment provides that the states cannot treat similarly situated people differently. Baker claimed that Tennessee's system of representation violated that Clause. For many decades, the Supreme Court had refused to hear such cases, the justices fearing they would be drawn into what they called a "political thicket" where they would be called upon to make decisions that they believed should properly be made only by elected legislators, or by someone else in the "political" branch of state government. But that all changed with Baker. The Court had not only agreed to hear the case; it had decided that the Tennessee system of apportionment of state legislative districts did deprive its citizens of equal protection. Fred was excited about the decision and the prospects it could bring, and his excitement was contagious.

He and I had groused about the inconveniences imposed upon us and our clients in Suffolk County, because virtually every public facility, including the trial courts to which we each often had to travel, were located in the County Seat of Riverhead, an "east end" town 50 miles away from my home and 25 miles away from Fred's. If I was on trial in Riverhead for five days, I put 500 miles on my car that week. Most of our clients—in fact, most of the county's residents—who had to appear in those courts, either for their own cases, or as witnesses, or for jury duty, lived in the County's "west end" and had the same problem.

Riverhead was one of five towns in the east end. It, and Southold, East Hampton, Southampton and Shelter Island, together contained only ten percent of the County's population. Ninety percent of the people in Suffolk lived in the five towns of the west end, but they had far from 90% of the voting power in the County's government.

The east enders were the ones who had political strength, and they made the most of it. The County's law-making body had been a ten-member Board of Supervisors for nearly 300 years. We literally had representation by town; each one, whether it had a large and growing population or a tiny static one, sent one representative—its "Supervisor," who, like a city mayor, was elected to serve as the chief executive of the town—to sit on the County Board as well. Our local arrangement was the same as the one Tennessee had for its state legislature.

Unless something changed, the east end, with ten per cent of the population but 50% of the vote, would always have a strangle-

MAKING LAW

hold on Suffolk's governing body. It was not rocket science to figure out that the east enders would place most of the County's vital facilities in their part of it, and they did. Long before the Baker decision, Fred and I had believed that the needs of our 90 percent of the County's population were being deliberately disregarded, and they were.

The 1960 census made it clear how bad the disparities were: the tiny Town of Shelter Island reported a population of 1,219 people, while Islip town in the west end was home to 172,000; yet each town had the same vote in county affairs—one. Fred proposed filing a case in the federal court in our district, to apply the Baker decision to our local government.

For a moment, I had an image of Fred, like some modern-day Don Quixote, tilting at the beautiful old East Hampton windmills which seemed to be emblematic of the east end, where they had existed since colonial days. Did I want to join him in what would be a bitter civil war between the two parts of the County?

Fred and I had a little rivalry going between us as well as a friendship, and I wondered, if he is Don Quixote, will I be Sancho Panza?

Bringing a case like the one Fred was proposing would have consequences for me. I had relationships with a lot of Republican officials who were benefiting in some way from the present system, and those relationships would, at the least, be thrown into turmoil.

I hesitated, but it was at first glance hard to see why the rule the Supreme Court had created in the Baker case should not logically apply to Suffolk County and other local governments that represented geographical areas rather than roughly equal numbers of people. I had read the Baker decision when it was announced and realized then what a dramatic step the Supreme Court had taken; it would no longer automatically avoid questions that it had classified as "political." But now I was being asked to join in filing another political case that could end up there, and just because the Court had decided that it would no longer avoid those questions didn't mean the Court would answer this one in the way we wanted.

Those closely following the Court knew that it had had a hard time with the Baker case itself. It was put off for a year because the justices could not agree, and when the decision was finally issued, it drew stinging dissents from Justices Felix Frankfurter and John Marshall Harlan. I wondered how likely it was that any of the justices would want to get into an even larger "thicket" at the local government level. A decision in our favor would require the reallocation of political power in many localities, and at that time the country had over 3,000 county governments. I did not know how many villages and cities there were.

America's tradition of having representation by geography was a serious obstacle. Suffolk's old system, like Tennessee's system, assumed that each local area had its unique characteristics and perspectives to contribute. That assumption may once have been valid, but the Supreme Court had now rejected the traditional notion of representing cities and towns instead of people. I figured there was a 50-50 chance of success (or perhaps less) in any lawsuit we might file. But potentially there was an exciting ending that made the choice almost irresistible: we might get to argue our case in the Supreme Court. We were very young: in March 1962, I was 29 years old and Fred was 27.

We agreed to try it.

Fred asked his friend Bill Bianchi, a young orchid-grower from Bellport, Long Island, and, like Fred, a Democrat, if he would become a plaintiff in a challenge to the Board of Supervisors system. I was then an enrolled Republican, and I put the same question to my longtime friend Quentin Sammis. He was a highly-respected insurance and real estate broker, his family had lived in Huntington since colonial days, and he was also a Republican. Both men were excited to be a part of the adventure.

Fred and I both thought (how wrong we were!) that our lawsuit would less likely be considered a partisan attack on the East-end Republicans who controlled the Board of Supervisors if one plaintiff was a Democrat and the other a Republican. Because of his political affiliation, Fred was not troubled that the case might bring grief to the Republicans. Because of mine, I was, but not enough to refuse to participate. We knew we had an unimaginable amount of work and a great deal of pressure ahead, and we would be putting ourselves on a very large stage. I thought it would be one of the greatest adventures of my career, and it was.

Throughout the country, a large number of politicians had to be digesting the implications of Baker for their area. Our filing of an actual case would galvanize people at the local government level everywhere to do the same, and soon there would be many others.

Fred and I drove to the federal court in Brooklyn on July 27, 1962, and filed Bianchi v. Griffing, and beat everybody else who was thinking of it. Ours was the first local government reapportionment case filed in the nation. "Griffing," whom we named as the first defendant in the title of the case, was Evans K. Griffing, the Supervisor of Shelter Island, the tiniest town in the county; he was first among equals as Chairman of the County Board of Supervisors, the body we were trying, figuratively, to blow up.

Over the next five years, I was calling and receiving telephone calls from attorneys from all over the country, with whom I would not otherwise have had any contact. Those special conversations came fast and furiously after the Supreme Court agreed in 1966 to hear our case in a one-line order that instantly became headline news throughout America.

However, as I thought, my participation in the case resulted in several testy talks with local Republicans. I had previously been considered a faithful Republican stalwart; in fact, the party had a fundraising group in our County that was actually named the "Stalwarts," to which I belonged. I had acted as a legal advisor for Republican leaders in in the town and the County, but any special status that I had enjoyed disappeared the moment the case was filed. I was no longer a stalwart, capitalized or otherwise. Arthur Cromarty, the County Republican Chairman, although himself a west-ender, publicly excoriated me as a "disloyal Republican." I knew that the west-end Supervisors, all Republicans, were just as frustrated as Fred and I were, that the east end Supervisors sitting with them on the County Board constantly flexed their political muscles at their expense, but they fell into line with Cromarty and publicly criticized the case and its perpetrators. No one was mollified that Quentin Sammis' name was on the legal papers—he was just another traitor to the party, like me.

In those times, political conflicts, even serious ones like the one between Cromarty and me, were more transactional than personal. He later went on to become a Supreme Court judge in our county, and always dealt with me fairly and cordially.

Not so for Griffing, the wiry and wily farmer, like Quentin Sammis from a venerable Suffolk County family. He thoroughly enjoyed casting his vote on the Board of Supervisors on behalf of his 1,218 neighbors on Shelter Island, while he watched Islip's Supervisor cast his one vote for his town's 172,000 residents. Griffing's position as Chairman of the Board gave him extra clout, which he was happy to use whenever possible. Our case was a serious threat to his power; if we won, he would thereafter merely be one of a larger number of county legislators sitting in a body which would no longer be attuned exclusively to his concerns and those of his five east end colleagues. The first time we encountered each other, at a court appearance in Brooklyn, he approached me, hostility written all over his face. His nose six inches from mine, he jabbed his finger into my chest and told me, "You're destroying this county! Why are you doing this?"

The federal court's random selection system popped up the name of the judge who would be assigned to the case: Walter Bruchhausen, 65 years old, who seemed somewhat stuffy, and from all indications fairly conservative. We felt that we could dilute Judge Bruchhausen's influence, as we had already decided to (legally) "pack" our court with two additional judges, invoking a little-known law, the "three-judge court" statute.

In certain types of cases, a lawyer could ask for a three-judge court—with two district judges and a third from the Court of Appeals—to hear it. Fred and I thought the best part of a three-judge court was that its decisions are appealed directly to the Supreme Court, bypassing the Circuit Court. Since other local government cases would surely be filed elsewhere in the country, Fred and I had just entered a race to the Supreme Court. The speediest litigant would have the honor of making new law—or die trying.

We wanted the Court not only to declare that the Suffolk Charter provision giving each town one vote, no matter how large or small its population, was unconstitutional, but also to order the County to adopt a new form of government, based on the "one man, one vote" principle the Supreme Court had adopted in the Baker case.

Fred and I discussed whether the case could qualify for a three-judge court because we were attacking the Suffolk County Charter, and you could only have a three-judge court if you were attacking a "statewide law." However, another law, the "County Law," was a statewide one, and it had a default provision that also provided for representation by town instead of by population. So, if the Suffolk County Charter was knocked out by the court, the county would still have the same kind of representation that we were claiming the Constitution prohibited. Nothing would change. For two enthusiastic young lawyers, this seemed a small procedural obstacle, and we were confident that asking for a special court so the case could quickly go to the Supreme Court was good strategy.

Our adversary was Stanley Corwin, a long-time deputy county attorney. I had known Stanley for years; he was an excellent lawyer, and a nice guy. He was an older man, quite gray, and always cordial in social encounters. But no one underestimated or misjudged him: he had bulldog tenacity, as well as considerable dramatic talent, all of which he mobilized against us.

Corwin called our case "ridiculous" and made a great show of indignation as he took Judge Bruchhausen through the many earlier cases in which the Supreme Court had declined to enter the "political thicket." Hey, we pointed out, that was then; the Supreme Court changed its mind: now there was Baker.

In April 1963, Judge Bruchhausen gave us each hope. He refused to dismiss the case himself, but gave Corwin an opportunity to make his motion to dismiss all over again, before a three-judge court.

The other two judges assigned to our case were District Judge John Dooling, a quiet, scholarly man, slight of stature, and extremely well-respected as a fair and thoughtful jurist; and Circuit Judge Leonard Moore, a well-liked former U.S. Attorney, who was regarded as conservative by disposition, but not dogmatic.

On September 30, 1963, the three judges would hear both Corwin's renewed dismissal motion and our motion for an injunction stopping the Supervisors from voting by town, as dictated by the county Charter. Fred argued the case that day.

The only courtroom that was big enough to accommodate a three-judge district court was the "ceremonial" one at the corner of Tillary Street and Cadman Plaza East in Brooklyn, ordinarily used for swearing in of new judges. That was the courtroom in

MAKING LAW

which Fred was himself sworn in as a federal judge some years later. It was nearly filled when our case was called.

Judges Moore and Dooling were engaged and interested, and Fred and I were pleased that they had been picked for the special court. We continued to worry about Judge Bruchhausen, who seemed to be impatient and a little bored. A 2-1 victory might be the best we could do.

When the decision came down 16 months later, Bruchhausen, to my surprise, agreed with his two colleagues. The unanimous Court cut to the chase and highlighted the widely disparate representation among Suffolk's towns:

> Little mathematical ingenuity is required to prove plaintiffs' thesis that the vote in county management affairs by the Supervisor from Shelter Island is representative of 1,300 persons whereas the equal vote of the supervisor of the Town of Islip is representative of over 172,000 persons. The individual vote ratio is over 100 to 1 in favor of Shelter Island and against Islip.

The rest of the decision made clear why it had taken them so long to write it. They had been asking themselves the key question that the case raised and set it out in their decision for all to see:

> "If county government within the states must conform to the Equal Protection Clause," they said, "then obviously, Baker v. Carr [and several other 1964 cases that applied Baker to legislatures in other states] call for action. But first there is the fundamental question of how far the judiciary should go?"

The judges answered their own question, by giving the county's officials the first opportunity to solve the problem. They were reluctant to impose their ideas of how a local government should be composed, but reserved the right to act if the County failed to do so.

That was a perfectly reasonable position for them to take, but since they imposed no specific order on the County, we could not yet take our dreamed-of direct appeal to the Supreme Court. Like the judges, we just had to wait.

And so we did, and another ten months went by, with nothing happening. So, in December 1965 we returned to court.

The County was now confronted with the possibility of direct action by the judges, and its political leaders got the message. A committee was appointed to make recommendations for the reapportionment of the county, a state official proposed adding one supervisor for each 100,000 of population, a spirited debate about "weighted voting" took place, and many meetings were held. It took five months for the committee to present four alternative plans to the Board of Supervisors, the very body whose makeup we were trying to change. These ranged from districting crossing town lines, to weighted voting within the existing town boundaries, to at-large voting. Local laws embodying various plans was introduced for consideration. Corwin made clear to the judges that he was not promising that any of the proposed plans would ever be adopted; he was unable to predict what his clients would do.

He was exactly right. The exercise invited by the Court had resulted in such a confusing whirl of conflicting ideas that no real consensus ever developed.

The judges finally lost patience. On June 15, 1966, they said, it was "obvious" that there must be "a change in the voting power of each of the present county supervisors so as to give to the voter more equal representation in his vote." They could no lon-

MAKING LAW

ger avoid dealing with local matters that are "thrust upon them," and imposed weighted voting on the Board of Supervisors, and directed that a permanent plan be presented by July 11th, less than one month later.

It had taken a long time, but the court had finally stopped use of the "one town, one vote" provision of the Suffolk County Charter. And all three judges had agreed.

So, as it turned out, it was the County that got to file a direct appeal to the Supreme Court. And, assuming the Court accepted the case, we would be there.

If the Supreme Court justices feel that a case does not qualify for direct appeal, they can dismiss it. If it seems that the correct procedure was followed, they "note probable jurisdiction."

Now, Fred and I were in a peculiar position; we had won our case, and we had the right to move to dismiss the appeal. If the Supreme Court granted our motion, our victory would become final. We would have won our case, but we would have lost our only likely chance ever to argue in the highest court in the land. Reluctantly, our personal egos had to take a back seat to the clients' interests, and with mixed feelings, we filed a traditional "Motion to Affirm and Dismiss." By then, following the filing of our case, there were so many lower court judges throughout the country who had now applied Baker v Carr to the local level of government that we could credibly argue that the question was now essentially settled; there was no longer a "substantial federal question" for the Court to decide.

We waited nervously to see whether the Supreme Court would take its first step into the local government reapportionment area.

One morning in early December 1966, a Western Union messenger entered my office and handed me a yellow envelope. Inside was a single sheet of paper, also yellow, to which several words were taped. Next to the name and docket number of our case, this simple phrase appeared:

RICHARD C. CAHN

"Probable jurisdiction noted."

Thus I learned that our motion to dismiss the County's appeal had been denied, but that our dream would come true: Fred and I (or at least one of us) would have the chance to argue a case in the highest court in the land, an opportunity that few lawyers have in a lifetime. Never before or since have I ever received a three-word note that gave me such a thrill.

How does a lawyer prepare for such a moment in his career? We were determined to do more than simply regurgitate all of the arguments in our lower court briefs. We thought it was critical in a case of this magnitude to give the Court all of the information the justices would need to understand the context of the case: the history of Suffolk County from the colonial era onward; how the Board of Supervisors came to be the governing body; the political forces and motivations of those arrayed against us; and the implications for other local forms of government nationwide.

The importance of the latter was underscored by several other Supreme Court orders issued the same day, agreeing to hear, together with our case, three other local government reapportionment cases.

One, Moody v. Flowers, involved the apportionment of a county board in Alabama, very much like ours. Another, Sailors v. Board of Education, dealt with the way school board members were chosen in Michigan; and the third, Dusch v. Davis, challenged a plan to merge Virginia City, Virginia with neighboring Princess Anne County and create a new governing body that would not give equal voices to the voters in different parts of the new city.

I started to call the lawyers in our new companion cases, and in a flood, letters and phone calls began to come in from lawyers representing counties and cities from everywhere, and also from lawyers representing citizen challengers to those local governments. Many cases had arisen, in Michigan, Florida, Texas, and in many other states. A sitting judge of the Michigan Supreme

MAKING LAW

Court wrote to me because his court had a case like ours to decide, and he had a number of questions he wanted to ask me; he and I corresponded for some weeks.

It was incredibly exciting to be inducted into this new and very special fraternity of lawyers (and judges) who were involved with cases like ours, and to have telephone conversations and letters back and forth that could deal with legal technicalities, like the Supreme Court's appellate jurisdiction, with historical and philosophical questions about how local governments in different parts of our country came to be the way they were, or whether there were other ways to organize a fair and constitutional representational scheme.

Many times I picked up my telephone and established a fellowship with a far-away lawyer whom I had never met, who was wrestling with the same legal and public policy questions that I was dealing with. The lawyer at the other end of the line might be a senior partner of one his state's elite "white shoe" law firms, or a single practitioner or municipal attorney in a tiny community I had never heard of; it didn't matter. That lawyer and I both had the same job to do—even those who were representing municipalities and therefore were part of the establishment that opposed what we were trying to do in the Bianchi case. We all had a shared mission, to clarify the law for local governments everywhere, and for the citizens they serve. We had the same legal issues to debate and the same Fourteenth Amendment to comply with. And we were all willing to help each other reason out how we would present our clients' cases, even, surprisingly, if we were on opposite sides of these questions. It was very helpful to learn from someone on the opposite side of the question what he thought his strongest legal arguments were.

There was an overwhelming shared sentiment among us all: we were involved in perhaps one of the most important cases that any of us would ever handle, and each of us had the possibility of being forever among the tiny fraction of American lawyers who argued before the Court. Fred and I and the lawyers in the three companion cases were already going to the legal Olympics, and some of the lawyers who spoke with me were on their way to the tryouts. But we all shared the same professional goals; we aspired to "make law," and to do so by demonstrating the highest level of legal skill of which we were each capable. The nation would be watching.

A case, Cargo v. Campbell, had recently been decided in New Mexico that involved the same weighted voting questions that I was going to argue in the Supreme Court; a little-known legislator had filed it against the state a few years before. I wanted to know more about the case, so I called the New Mexico Attorney General's office to see if someone in that office could answer a few questions. I knew courtesies would be extended to me and I would be connected with a staff attorney who would fill me in on its details.

A male voice answered, "This is the Attorney General."

New Mexico is a small state, but who would believe the AG answers his own phone?

I asked him if there was anyone in his office who could tell me about Cargo v. Campbell. There was a silence, and then he said, "Well, I could tell you a lot about it myself, but hold on a minute, there's somebody here in my office who can tell you more."

Another voice came on the phone: "Good Morning. This is Governor Cargo." This was the David Cargo who had brought the case that I was asking about; unbeknownst to me, it had propelled him to election as New Mexico's governor. We were only four years apart in age; he was 38.

Well, that was unexpected, I thought. There's a down-to-earth guy!

The first thing I wanted to know was how the judges in his case had reacted to his arguments about weighted voting. And

MAKING LAW

within minutes, the Governor of New Mexico and I were in a detailed discussion about whether weighted voting would satisfy the requirements of the Fourteenth Amendment. We were separated by more than 2,000 miles, but during that phone conversation, we were just two young lawyers talking to one another about the pros and cons of legal arguments in a new and novel case. I thought Cargo was enjoying the exchange as much as I was.

In some intangible way, that conversation, followed by an exchange of letters, drove home to me the high stakes in the case. When would I ever otherwise have had the occasion to get into an intense, unplanned, and lengthy telephone discussion with the Governor of one of our sister states? I was energized as I continued my preparation for oral argument in the high court.

One final arrangement was of critical importance to Fred and me. Normally, the Supreme Court only allows one lawyer to argue for each set of clients. And, although we both pretended to make light of it, Fred and I had appeared in the lower court as joint attorneys for both Bianchi and Sammis, and each of us was wondering how we would decide which of us would be arguing the case. We each believed that we would soon have to face a painful choice and an even more painful reality: one of us would rise as the case was called; the other would be reduced to sitting next to the lectern and handing notes to the one who would argue. I was thinking we might have to resolve the issue by a coin toss.

An unlikely group of characters came to our rescue: Supervisors from the five heavily populated west-end towns, ironically, all Republicans, broke with their party leader Cromarty, who had so publicly attacked Quentin Sammis and me for bringing the case. They realized, particularly in light of the wildly favorable publicity our case was enjoying in the press, that it was in their political interest to support us. Their constituents, Republicans and Democrats alike, were all now clamoring for greater representation for the west end in county government.

So, the five Republican Supervisors, possibly hating every moment of it, asked me to petition the Supreme Court for permission to file a friend-of-the-court brief in their behalf, and to seek separate oral argument. I was extremely happy to do so, and in February 1967, two months before our scheduled argument date, the Court granted my request. Fred and I would each have our personal day in court; there would be two oral argument spots for our side of the case. When the Court published its calendar, the four reapportionment cases were scheduled to span two days, Monday and Tuesday, April 17-18, 1967. We would be the third case to be argued, and were scheduled for Tuesday morning, so we would have the luxury of sitting in on Monday's arguments to see how the justices were reacting.

The trip to Washington was a grand affair for my family. Perry Lippitt, the Marshall of the Court, reserved seven seats in the courtroom for my family and for Quentin Sammis and his wife. My mother, two years a widow, came to Washington to see me argue before the high court, sadly reflecting that my father, who had regaled us for so many years with tales of his own court appearances, had not lived to see that day. Vivian was preparing, as she had done on other occasions before, to hold her breath for the entire time I was on my feet, willing me not to make a mistake. And my dear mother-in-law Razunia added a special dimension to the experience, with her own brand of contagious excitement that she, once a 12-year-old immigrant from the Ukraine newly arrived in this land of promise, would now watch her son-in-law argue an important case in America's highest court.

The oral argument was complicated by the procedural issue that we worried about in the early weeks of planning for the lawsuit: was it proper to have convened a three-judge court since the Suffolk County Charter was not a statute of state-wide application?

Unfortunately for us, the United States Solicitor General had weighed in on this question, and we were not happy about what he said. The Solicitor General has been called the "tenth justice" on the nine-member Supreme Court, officially advising the Court of the government's views, which are given great weight by the justices. One of the things the Solicitor General does is to point out things that the lawyers for the parties may not have highlighted in their briefs. Although we covered the point in our briefs, we had hoped not to be required to dwell on the propriety of the three-judge court, which was the underpinning of the Supreme Court's jurisdiction. That turned out to be an idle hope.

Fred and I went to Washington two months before the case would be heard, to write our briefs without distraction. I met Assistant Solicitor General Francis X. Beytagh then; I remember him as tall, well-tailored, and cordial, and completely open about the position the government would take in its brief. I was happy to hear him say that he completely agreed that the "one man, one vote" principle should be extended to elective county legislatures, but not at all when he told us that he and his colleagues strongly believed that this was not a proper case for a three-judge court.

That was how Fred and I came to divide up the oral argument; he would address the three-judge court issue and I would argue the merits of the Equal Protection claim and discuss weighted voting, the remedy that the three-judge court had imposed upon the county. When the justices actually began to question us, the division between our selected topics considerably blurred, but I still felt I got the best of that bargain.

The Sailors case was heard on Monday morning, and we were there. We checked in with the Clerk's office, and to my delight, I ran into Professor Rodell. He and I caught up on each other's lives, and he expressed dismay that he had to return to New Haven for a class the next day, and wouldn't be able to hear our argument. I wondered afterwards if he was still holding classes at Mory's, but I never asked. He made me promise I'd tell him afterwards how it went. I felt that our surprise encounter was a good omen.

The personnel in the Supreme Court Clerk's office were among the friendliest and most helpful of those in any court I have ever encountered. They had prepared Court credentials for Fred and me and gave us explicit instructions about the customs of the Court, where to sit when we were "on deck", and how many minutes of argument remaining were indicated by each colored light on the speaker's lectern.

Gene Levitt, a Huntington lawyer whose age was somewhere between my father's and mine, had long been a wonderful family friend; in a way I had inherited him from my parents. He traveled from Long Island to share the thrill we were about to experience. Perry Lippett, the Marshall, told him he wouldn't need a ticket; all he had to do was tell one of the Court's officers that he was a member of the Supreme Court bar (which he was) and he would be admitted to the counsel section of the courtroom.

Since our argument would span Tuesday's lunch hour, Lippett's office even took our lunch orders. The Court would break for 30 minutes at noon, and there would be no time to eat elsewhere. When the argument broke sharply the next day, our lunches were waiting for us in a small room behind the bench. Never before or since have I encountered the level of respect, warmth and civility on the part of court clerks and staff anywhere that I experienced those two days in April 1967 and during the weeks leading up to it.

On Tuesday, we were at the Court nearly an hour before the scheduled 10 a.m. start. I was determined to rise to the occasion; my mind was racing. I desperately needed to hold on to every detail

MAKING LAW

of the facts and every nuance of the case precedents. How many times had I formulated and reframed what I wanted to say, trying each time I silently went over it in my mind to make it shorter and more persuasive?

The day before I had noted the justices' interest in the kind of functions performed by the various government bodies involved in these four cases; several of the justices made it clear that they thought the "one man, one vote" rule should only apply to bodies performing legislative functions, so after Monday's arguments, I had telephoned the clerk of the Board of Supervisors back in Riverhead, who recited for me (again!) the specific legislative duties the supervisors performed. I had forgotten some of those details and knew that at least one of us would be heavily questioned about what the Board did.

Fred began his argument with a defense of the three-judge court and was promptly challenged by the Justices. Beytagh had argued the day before and again that morning, emphasizing the government's doubts about the Court's jurisdiction in both our case and in the Alabama one. Since I was to argue the far easier merits of "one man, one vote," I was happy to hear Beytagh on both days make my point for me, advising the justices that the government's position was that the Constitution required the "one man, one vote" to apply to the local levels of government. He said the issue in the case was "of importance to millions of Americans," and their "fundamental right to fair and equal treatment in the electoral process at the local level."

The Supreme Court always addresses any jurisdictional questions before it rules on the merits of a case. It became clear as our oral arguments continued that the justices were finding it difficult to believe that our case directly or indirectly involved a law of statewide application. It now looked like we would lose the procedural point and find ourselves back before the lower courts. Bianchi would lose its chance to be the leading case on this subject.

RICHARD C. CAHN

When I later read the transcript, I saw that Fred had explained our jurisdictional argument well; but while he was delivering it I had been thinking more about what I would say than listening carefully to him. Then it was my turn.

My part of the oral argument was easy by comparison. The government had already endorsed our position. There were no obvious mishaps, other than that Justice Black mispronounced my name "Can" to rhyme with "tin can". Some of the Justices were clearly concerned that this case might open the courthouse doors too widely, since there were at the time over 3,000 counties across the nation, as compared to just 50 states, but I had the sense that we probably had a majority of the justices with us. I did not believe we had all of them, by any means.

Justice Fortas had asked Fred a number of questions about what legislative functions the Board of Supervisors performed; Fred mentioned a couple of things and then went back to his critical assignment to defend the three-judge court. Since I had just the day before reviewed those very items with the Board's clerk and made notes, I began by reeling off all the "legislative" duties that the Board performed, and received a hearty "Thank you, Mr. Cahn," from Justice Fortas.

There was an arcane discussion with Justices White, Brennan, Black and Clark about weighted voting. The lower court had directed the County to adopt a new plan that would align the representation of each town on the Board with its population. The County had "evened out" the representation among the towns by creating additional supervisors for the more populous ones.

The "weighted voting" argument had been very difficult to prepare. Until I began to write my part of the briefs, I had no idea that this case would take me so far out of the realm of law. I had consulted with Layman Allen, my mathematically talented law school classmate at Yale who had invented and marketed a logic

MAKING LAW

game that he called "Whiffenproofs," and with Thomas Kurtz, the head guru at Dartmouth's Kiewit Computer Center, to learn how mathematicians analyzed weighted vote systems, so I could better understand whether they helped or hindered citizens' right to fair representation. And I had discussed that very subject with New Mexico Governor Cargo. Now, all of that preparation proved to be valuable.

Justice White asked me whether there was any difference between having two supervisors in a large town and having one supervisor with twice the vote. I thought it was a good sign that the mechanics of solving the representation problem were of interest to at least four Justices: I thought that might mean that they agreed that a problem did exist, and knew that at some point they would have to figure out what kind of remedy was appropriate.

Justice Black asked me if there was an argument for upholding the long history of representation by towns before the ratification of the Constitution, and I struck a blow against an "originalist" interpretation of the Constitution by telling him that I did not think history was a consideration in the case because times had changed greatly since 1787. Then Justice Brennan chimed in and pointed out the obvious point that there was no 14th Amendment in 1787. Chief Justice Warren asked few questions, but was attentive and unfailingly gracious to us all.

My allotted time expired; the green light on the lectern turned first to orange, and then to red, but the Justices still continued to ask questions, keeping me at the lectern for 30 minutes, twice my allotted time. I felt good.

I picked up two quill pens from our counsel table and handed one to my friend Gene; the day's hearing list and the ID card that the Court had issued for my appearance went into my briefcase. I turned away, left the courtroom and emerged into the sunshine. I was excited and elated, but my mind was blank; I couldn't remember anything I had said. As I walked down the marble steps a radio reporter from Huntington radio station WGSM strode alongside, thrust a microphone and tape recorder in my face, and asked me for my reactions. I told him I was hopeful about the result. Luckily, he didn't ask me to recount any parts of the argument itself. I later recovered my memory and reconstructed the arguments in my promised letter to Fred Rodell.

The news cycle soon ended, as did the flurry of interviews with the press and the long conversations briefing each of the West end Supervisors. My emotions returned to normal, excitement crowded out by the pressures of new cases, and by the necessity of performing the usual chores in our small law office.

Years later, my College opened the Rauner Library in Hanover, N.H. as a repository for original manuscripts and letters. On one of my visits to the campus, I asked to see the collection of Daniel Webster's letters relating to The Dartmouth College case which he argued before the Supreme Court in 1819. In a string-bound portfolio I found the original letters that Webster had written 148 years before to his client, Francis Brown, Dartmouth's then President, and to other lawyers interested in the event, including the renowned American jurist, Chancellor Kent. In his neat, flowing and still readable handwriting, Webster described and expressed his opinion about each lawyer's contribution—including his own—to the arguments in the case, and speculated about how the justices would likely vote.

Webster's case rescued the small college that I was to attend 130 years later from an attempted takeover by New Hampshire's Legislature. Webster beat back the State's attempt to seize ownership and control of the College by ousting its private trustees, men in the direct line of succession from those receiving the College's original Charter in 1769 from Royal Governor John Wentworth of the Colony of New Hampshire.

MAKING LAW

The Dartmouth College Case became one of the most famous Constitutional law cases in American history, establishing that the government had no right to interfere with contract rights.

As I held Daniel Webster's original letters in my hand, I realized I was hearing a war story from a hero from the past, in his own words:

> Our college cause has been argued. I have no accurate knowledge of the manner in which the judges are divided. The Chief and Washington, I have no doubt are with us, Duval and Todd perhaps against us; the other three holding up. I cannot much doubt but that Story will be with us in the end, and I think we have much more than an even chance for one of the others. I think we shall finally succeed.

I could relate to Webster. I, too, had gone through his experience, worrying about how each justice would vote, and what the odds were that we would win. On the day of my appearance, not quite 35 years old, I had virtually skipped down the grand marble steps in front of the Supreme Court. As the *three days* of arguments in the Dartmouth case continued, Webster, then also in his 30s, had become steadily more optimistic that he would win. "On the whole," he said at the end, "we have reason to keep up our courage."

Like Webster, I had felt the weight of history on my shoulders. I held his handwritten letters in my hands, and relived my own experience that day in Washington years earlier: I could now recall the faces of the justices, the questions they asked of me, and the mind-freezing moments as I raced to organize the mass of information I had packed into my brain. And I also remembered trying in real time to sort these judges out in my mind, divine the motivation for each question, and intuit whether the questioner was trying to puncture my argument, or whether he was really an ally prodding me to answer a question one of his skeptical colleagues may have put to him beforehand.

What I had said then to the United States Supreme Court was trifling in comparison to the words of Daniel Webster, one of the greatest lawyers and orators in American history, but I felt joined to him, a brother lawyer, as I touched the brittle pages that had actually been in his fingers a century and a half before. The special mission that lawyers share and cherish, transcends not only geography but also time.

We did win our case, but less dramatically than I had hoped. In May, the Justices said that the County's direct appeal was procedurally improper because this was not a three-judge court case. Beytagh had charted the course, and the Court had followed.

So, a year later, it was the Second Circuit in Manhattan that delivered our victory.

But we didn't "make law." Lawyers from Texas beat us back to the Supreme Court. On April 1, 1968, almost one year after we had argued in Washington, the Supreme Court decided Avery v. Midland County, Texas, extending the "one man, one vote" principle to county government. I remembered that one of the many letters that had sought to exchange information before I went to Washington came from F. H. Pannill, one of Midland County's lawyers. I had given him a copy of the legal brief that we had filed, which contained our arguments in favor of "one man, one vote," the same arguments that were later presented by Hank Avery's lawyers as they argued against Mr. Pannill in that case.

No procedural issue had interfered with the joy of Avery's lawyers, because their case had come to the Supreme Court from the Texas state court, and there was no three-judge court problem. Four days after the Supreme Court acted, our final victory came from the Circuit Court in Manhattan.

MAKING LAW

Our odyssey, now six-years long, was over. Fred and I had presented a question of great public importance to the nation's highest Court, and we ended up on the right side of history. We could claim a role in shaping an important principle of American law, but only as a footnote. Remembering Justice Fortas' questions, I was glad to see that in the Sailors decision, the justices noted that the Suffolk County Board of Supervisors was a good example of a local body that exercised legislative powers.

Fred had invited me to share an exciting personal and professional adventure, helping to bring better representation to citizens of malapportioned counties like ours, and it all happened. We filed the first local apportionment case, and each of us had the rare and elevating experience of personally arguing a case to the Supreme Court. I had had an unexpected glimpse into the breadth and talent of the American legal profession. Those conversations dramatized for me the dedication of so many lawyers, regardless of where they live and practice, or their station in life, to the high ideals of the American justice system.

Earl Warren later said that the reapportionment cases were among the most important that the Court decided in his time as Chief. He had to fight hard for the result he wanted, winning the support of only four colleagues in the Avery case. Justice Stewart's pointed dissenting opinion showed how troubled he was: he thought his colleagues had "betrayed insensitivity to the appropriate dividing lines between judicial and political functions under our constitutional system." Justice Fortas, also dissenting, was still looking closely at the types of functions the local unit of government performed, insisting that the Court should not "simplistically" apply "one man, one vote" rule to all local bodies with governing powers. And the Chief lost Justice Harlan as well. The dissenters were troubled by a startling fact that these cases had uncovered: beyond the 3,000 counties in the nation, there were nearly *80,000* local bodies having some sort of governing powers. The justices of the highest court in the land had made a policy decision with enormous consequences. And, at least at the time of this writing, it appears that that policy decision is not likely to be set aside by the Court.

During the last several years, it did appear that the Court might also come to grips with partisan gerrymandering, which Justice Souter in a dissenting opinion had once pointed out was a way, other than malapportionment, to "skew political results."

A series of gerrymandering cases, sequels to the reapportionment cases of the 1960s, came to the Court in 2018, but the Court sent them back to the lower courts for further proceedings, raising hopes on the part of liberals that the contours and extent of the rights of Americans to fair elections would ultimately be more fully protected.

The battle that the Court reluctantly joined in 1962 with Baker v Carr, that the Bianchi case helped bring to local governments, and that Justice Souter had wanted to extend to gerrymandering, did return to the Court for the 2018-1019 Term. By then, four solid conservatives were firmly in place, with the hopes of the *conservatives* now raised by the expectation that Chief Justice Roberts would join them and *validate* gerrymandering.

On June 27, 2019, Chief Justice Roberts did not disappoint them, siding with the four conservatives in a stunning decision. Even though they conceded that the gerrymanders in question "involved blatant examples of partisanship driving districting decisions," that is "incompatible" with democratic principles, they held that claims against gerrymandering "present political questions beyond the reach of the federal courts."

Justice Kagan issued a stinging dissent:

> For the first time ever, this Court refuses to remedy a constitutional violation because it thinks the

task beyond judicial capabilities ... [a]nd not just any constitutional violation. The partisan gerrymanders in these cases deprived citizens of the most fundamental of their constitutional rights: the rights to participate equally in the political process, to join with others to advance political beliefs, and to choose their political representatives, ... debased and dishonored our democracy, turning upside-down the core American idea that all governmental power derives from the people. ... If left unchecked, gerrymanders like the ones here may irreparably damage our system of government.

Thus, the Supreme Court turned another page in our political history. Who knows whether a future court will reverse that gerrymandering decision, because important issues like this one, are like General Douglas MacArthur's "old soldiers" who "never die." It may be that gerrymandering is beyond the reach of the federal courts, but three North Carolina *state* court judges have issued a 357-page decision striking down that state's legislative districts as partisan gerrymandering under North Carolina's constitution. We may be seeing a rebirth of state court involvement in important political issues that the nation's highest court has declined to resolve. They will not go away.

7

THERE'S A MURDERER OUT THERE. THE GOVERNMENT DOESN'T CARE.

Fifty years ago, sometime after midnight on February 17, 1970, two little girls and their mother were killed in their home on a U. S. military base surrounded by tight security. There was no sign of an intrusion, a neighbor's watchdog failed to bark, and the identity of the perpetrator(s) was unknown.

Six hundred miles away, my family was celebrating the birth of our second son, Daniel. As I watched my young wife embrace him, I did not know that two years later. I would be drawn into the horrifying events that had ended the lives of another young wife and her children earlier that same day, crimes that, it seemed, would never be prosecuted.

These events took place in a small house at 544 Castle Drive, on the United States Army post at Ft. Bragg, North Carolina, which served as officer's quarters for Captain Jeffrey MacDonald, age 26, Princeton graduate, physician and Green Beret. He lived there with his wife Colette, 25, who was pregnant with a son, and their two daughters, Kimberly, 5, and Kristen, 2.

Shortly before 4 a.m. on February 17th, MacDonald's strained voice came through the base operator's headphones; there had been an attack at the caller's home, and people were dead or badly injured. Military Police responded and found Colette's bloody body, sprawled on the floor of the master bedroom with her husband's pajama top covering her chest; on the headboard of the bed was written the word PIG, in blood. The two girls were dead, each in her own bed, neatly tucked under the covers which when pulled back revealed that both children had been bludgeoned and stabbed in what one person at the crime scene described as "massive overkill."

MacDonald lay, alive and conscious, on the master bedroom floor near his wife's body. He later told investigators that he had been asleep on the living room couch and was awakened by her screams. Four bizarre intruders were standing over him: a woman with a floppy hat, chanting "Acid is groovy, kill the pigs;" a large muscular black man; and two other hippie types. From the master bedroom, he heard his wife's voice: "Jeff, Jeff, why are they doing this to me?" He tried to rise from the couch, but his arms were tangled in his pajama top and he was unable to defend himself. The black man used his two arms to raise a baseball bat-like club high and struck him with it on the head; then he felt a sharp pain and realized he had been stabbed in the right chest. He lost consciousness and awakened later to a silent house. Crawling down the hall on hands and knees from the living room to the master bedroom, he discovered Colette's body, attempted to revive her, placed his torn pajama top on her chest "to keep her warm," then made his way to his daughters' bedrooms and tried to resuscitate them too. All the members of his family were dead—except him. He entered the bathroom, examined his own wounds, washed himself off, and telephoned for assistance.

He said he had no idea why he was the only member of the family left alive.

There was an eerie resemblance to the savage killings of actress Sharon Tate and four friends at her home in Los Angeles carried out by the Charles Manson "family" six months earlier. The working hypothesis of Army investigators was that these were "copycat murders."

From Colette's birth, her mother Mildred Stevenson cherished her in a very special way. She and her husband Edward badly wanted children, and before Colette was born, Mildred had two other "Colettes," both stillborn. When her third daughter was born, she survived, and they named her "Colette," too. She was the Colette who was murdered on February 17, 1970.

Colette was 11 and her brother Robert was 16 when their father Edward Stevenson, died. A gentle, well-liked man, Edward owned a small restaurant in Patchogue, Long Island, a popular gathering spot for the community. Long-time patrons crowded into his restaurant to mourn his passing with Mildred and their two children.

Mildred was still a widow when Colette entered her teen years. Alfred "Freddy" Kassab had not yet appeared on the scene, and the only male in the household was Robert. A young man, whom the family knew since he and Colette had attended Bay Avenue Elementary School together, began to hang around their house. Mildred asked him if he wanted a job mowing their lawn and he said yes. He was older than Colette by seven months, and their grade school friendship had continued.

His name was Jeffrey MacDonald.

Jeffrey and Colette attended Patchogue High School together, and their relationship blossomed. At 18, they both graduated; Jeffrey went off to Princeton and Colette to Skidmore. Within two years, in September 1963, they were married. Colette left college to be with her new husband, and the following April their daughter Kimberly was born.

In the meantime, Mildred's life dramatically changed. In 1960, six years after Edward's death, Mildred had married Alfred Kassab, a Canadian who had graduated from McGill University and become a member of OSS. During World War II he parachuted behind the German lines six times to contact the French Resistance. When I met him in 1972, he was blunt and gruff. But during the earlier years, "Freddy", as he was called by Mildred and her children, was different: Robert said he was "the gentlest and kindest of men." When he came into the family, he and Colette, then 16, bonded not as stepfather and stepdaughter, as Freddy emphasized to me. He had trouble holding his emotions back as he told me that they could not have loved each other more if they had been father and daughter by blood.

When Colette and Jeffrey married, Mildred and Freddy were delighted. They saw Jeff then as "an all-American boy who could charm the birds out of the trees." But when Kimberly was three years old and Colette was pregnant with Kristen, Mildred went to stay with Colette for a week to help out, and returned to Long Island with a dramatically different feeling.

Robert remembers his mother returning to Long Island and describing Jeffrey then as a "harsh, directive male," who was "dominant" in the marriage, "ordering" Colette around. When he next saw his sister, Robert also thought she was "totally cowed."

Robert and Jeff had disliked each other from the beginning. But Freddy was not ready to write Jeff off; he saw Jeff's abilities, intelligence and charm. Even Mildred's reservations about Jeff softened after Kristen, the second child, was born. In the immediate aftermath of the Ft. Bragg murders, Jeff's survival was the only bright spot in the Kassabs' life.

So, when Army investigators announced that MacDonald was a suspect in the murders, confined him to quarters and charged him with the murders, Freddy reacted with outrage. He began to call reporters, using colorful and forceful language—which he invited the press to quote—to protest what the Army was doing. The reporters loved the story, and Freddy's words were widely published.

Mildred and Freddy felt no one knew Jeff better than they did. For months, they never seriously entertained the possibility that their son-in-law could have committed these horrific crimes. Freddy once wondered out loud whether Jeff could have done so, and Mildred shot back, referring to what had happened at Christmas, less than two months before the killings: "a man who bought his children a pony couldn't do this," she said.

Freddy later wrote, "There was a staunch," [he meant "stench"], because the Army was "holding my son-in-law on suspicion of having killed his wife and daughters. What they alleged was not only impossible, it was unthinkable. I knew Jeff. A bright, determined doctor, a wonderful husband and adoring father."

In an unpublished writing called "Vendetta," Freddy wrote how he and Mildred had "gathered petitions at church meetings and shopping malls on Long Island ... We got more than 2,000 names to petition the Army" to "go after the real criminals and stop hounding poor Jeff. It wasn't easy getting the names because a surprising number of people wouldn't sign: they thought Jeff was guilty."

The saga of the Army's foray into a possible prosecution of Jeffrey MacDonald unfolded before I met the Kassabs, but it shaped everything that happened later.

Under the Uniform Code of Military Justice, charging an Army officer with a major crime requires holding an "Article 32" proceeding to determine whether a general court martial should be convened to try the accused. In MacDonald's case, the presiding officer, Col Warren V. Rock, gaveled such a proceeding to order on May 15, 1970, and it continued for 25 days. The hearing was closed to the public and featured testimony from the Army's Criminal Investigation Division (CID), but the bizarre highlight of the Article 32 proceeding was unexpected testimony from none other than the accused. MacDonald, although he was not legally required to do so, made a fateful decision to take the witness stand himself.

MAKING LAW

Freddy was briefly called to testify, but neither he nor Mildred had any first-hand information about the events of February 17, and all they knew about what other witnesses had said, was what Jeff told them in nightly phone calls that he made after the close of the hearing each day. They eagerly awaited his daily narratives.

Night after night, he reported that the proceeding was going "extremely well." Before the hearing, he had told them what he knew of the events of the fatal night, and now he recited what the witnesses in the Article 32 proceeding were testifying to, and how the physical evidence corroborated what he was telling them. The Kassabs were elated; nothing they heard from Jeff caused either of them to question his innocence.

At the conclusion of the Article 32 proceeding on October 13, 1970, their wish was granted. Col. Rock found no reasonable basis to charge MacDonald and, going far beyond the scope of his authority, he gratuitously announced that the charges were "untrue." Jeff was released from custody.

It was a cause to celebrate, but Freddy did not let his campaign against the Army die. He now stewed, privately and publicly, about what the Army had "done to Jeff," and soon he added a more urgent complaint: now, after Jeff had been cleared, the Army had apparently decided to ignore these crimes altogether: it was doing absolutely nothing to identify and prosecute the real killer. Freddy accelerated his calls to the media and press reporters on his growing "contact list," and his message got out as he had intended; the press found Freddy's biting comments to be excellent "copy," and reported them at length. Everyone was wondering what the Army was going to do next—if anything.

Freddy's thoughts turned back to Jeff and he began to pressure the Army to grant him a hardship discharge because of the "tragic loss of his family." The Army did not resist. In December, 1970, 11 months after the murders, MacDonald was discharged, a free man. He left North Carolina and traveled west to practice medicine in a small hospital in Long Beach, California.

MacDonald believed that his troubles were over and began to take steps to rebuild his life. He told Freddy and Mildred that he was beginning to date again. They understood and did not object.

However, the relationship oddly changed. Formerly, MacDonald had been eager to tell his in-laws every detail of the Article 32 testimony, but now he kept forgetting to authorize the Army to release the transcript to them, which he had promised he would do. The Army would not release it to them without his consent.

Freddy desperately wanted to read it. With his background in intelligence, he thought he might find in the mass of Article 32 evidence some clue to the real killers that the Army investigators had missed. Finally, MacDonald gave his authorization, and in November the Kassabs received 18 volumes of the record.

Freddy's ability to commit to memory every detail that Jeffrey had previously related to them was about to become a big problem for MacDonald. Since the day of the crimes, Freddy and Mildred had thought about nothing else. They wanted every scrap of information they could get. So, when they finally received the transcript, Freddy devoured it in less than a week.

It was unbelievably shocking.

The story their son-in-law had related to them in those nightly phone calls was completely at odds with the evidence presented at the Army hearing. Freddy couldn't believe what he was seeing and kept going back to the transcript to be sure he had read it correctly. He had. He couldn't understand how Col. Rock had reached the decision to dismiss the charges. When I finally got to read the Article 32 record myself, I shared Freddy's consternation.

Mildred had tried to read it, but found it too painful and soon put it down, but not before she reached exactly the same conclusion as Freddy had: either MacDonald had committed the murders himself, or he was covering up for someone else.

MAKING LAW

Mildred had a special reason to be devastated by that conclusion. Two weeks before the killings, Colette had telephoned her, sounding distressed; she wanted to come up to Long Island for a visit. Mildred, not realizing that there was any urgency to the situation, put her daughter off—some repair work was being done at their house—and told Colette it would be better if she came up at a later date. To the day of her own death, Mildred felt guilty, believing that if she had acceded to her daughter's wish to come north, the murders would never have happened.

The emotional impact of the transcript, which laid out graphically the most intimate and horrifying details of the manner in which their loved ones had met their deaths, would have crushed most victims' families; but infinitely adding to Freddy and Mildred's pain was the horrifying and previously unthinkable realization that, from start to finish, the narrative of their son-in-law, whom they had dearly loved, was contrived and false.

There was an unusual circumstance in this case: each member of the family had a different blood type, and that made it possible to reconstruct the movements of each of the victims and of MacDonald himself, by preparing a "map" of the apartment showing where each person's blood had been shed. One day in my office, Freddy drew that map from memory and explained it to me.

The Army's transcript set out the scientific evidence: MacDonald had said his pajama top was torn during the struggle in the living room and that he had placed it on Colette's body before he went to check on his daughters, yet there were no signs of a struggle in the living room, and marks on the ceiling and walls of the master bedroom, among other things, showed that a struggle had taken place there. The pocket had become detached from the pajama and was also found in the master bedroom. Fibers from the pajama top were also found near Colette's body in the master bedroom, and forensic testing showed that the pajama top was not torn when soaked with Colette's blood.

On the bed and floor of Kristen's bedroom, was a large quantity of type O blood, that of Kristen. On the wall to the left of Kristen's body, which was found in her bed, several spatters of blood of Colette's type were located in a pattern suggesting that some instrument bearing Colette's blood was swung in a downward motion toward the bed, although she was not struck with the bludgeon. Cursory inspection of Kristen's body at first seemed to indicate that she was murdered in her sleep and did not have her position changed to any appreciable degree. The position of the baby's bottle, containing a small amount of chocolate milk, seemed to lend credence to this assumption. However, it was discovered that Kristen was stabbed in her chest and in her back in motions which caused the knife and ice pick to penetrate straight into her body and not at an angle. MacDonald told investigators that he attempted to give mouth-to-mouth resuscitation to Kristen, but he did not recall placing the baby bottle in front of her face. The inference was inescapable that after she was murdered, the position of her body was changed, and she was covered up with the bedding and the baby bottle placed close to her face. Colette's type blood was found in large quantities on the sheet at Kristen's hip, indicating that Colette was present in the room while bleeding severely.

Three bloody footprints in Colette's blood type and matching the size and configuration of her husband's feet, were found on the floor exiting from Kristen's room.

Kimberly's body was found in her bed, with the left side of her face resting against the pillow, and examination of her body showed that she had received at least one blow to the left side of her face, which lacerated her cheek, fractured her nose and pushed it to the right. Her blood was soaked into the master bedroom rug. where some of her bloody hairs were also found. Stains in her blood and that of her mother were found on the hallway floor in front of Kimberly's bedroom door; all of this evidence indicated that she had been attacked in the master bedroom, and transported back to her own room and placed into her bed. Fibers from Jeffrey's pajama top were found on the underside of the top sheet in Kimberly's bed; another fiber from the pajama, together with a splinter from a wooden club identified as having struck Colette and Kimberly, were found behind the pillow on the right side of the bed.

MacDonald's denial of his own involvement required you to believe that it was not he, but rather a group of murderous hippies, who had mortally wounded Kimberly in the master bedroom and then moved her body to her own bedroom, carefully tucking it into her own bed, and that someone from the same group of perpetrators had stabbed Kristen while she slept in her bed, and then rearranged her body. No one could find any basis to believe that strangers to the family—indeed, that anyone other than MacDonald, the only other person present in the house, would have done either of those two things.

MacDonald denied that an ice pick of the type found at the crime scene (and identified as one of the murder weapons) was from the family's quarters, yet Pamela Kalin, the teenage babysitter next door, and Mildred Kassab both knew that it was kept in a kitchen drawer because each had used it. (At the trial, MacDonald finally admitted that it belonged to the family).

Despite MacDonald's claim of four intruders, there was no objective evidence of any invasion. It was raining, yet there was no foreign material such as grass, mud or wet spots anywhere in the home. The Kalins, immediate neighbors, "heard no sounds of a commotion, screaming, loud voices or any other abnormal noise." Their watchdog always barked at strangers, but that night was the proverbial dog that did not bark.

Then there was the disparity between the number (which kept changing) and severity of MacDonald's wounds and the attacks upon his family members. He had initially claimed that he had suffered 19 wounds, but medical examination had only revealed seven, of which six were superficial and the seventh could have been self-inflicted. Then he said he had sustained "Ten ice-pick wounds to the abdomen" that no doctor ever saw, and that would have been physically impossible for an individual to receive while in a sitting position. The number of his wounds further increased to 22 when he later appeared on the Dick Cavett Show, but none of his blood was ever found in the living room.

There was no plausible explanation for any of this.

The only viable conclusion, which Freddy and Mildred reached with sinking stomachs, was that MacDonald had concocted the whole story. There were no intruders at 544 Castle Drive that night, and their son-in-law, the father of their grandchildren to whom he had indeed given a pony weeks before, was the brutal killer whose identity that they had been trying to divine for more than eight months. The alternative possibility, that he was covering up for another person, had no evidence to support it, and they quickly rejected it.

Mildred left it to Freddy to explain the evidence to the press, and he did just that. Although his words were emphatic and he seemed at times to be barely controlling his anger, he marshaled the evidence with a prosecutor's skills, reciting from memory the incremental clues that to both of them proved "MacDonald's" guilt. They would never again refer to him as "Jeff."

They were deeply shaken by what they had discovered. In "Vendetta," Freddy's unpublished essay, he wrote about their painful transformation from being their son-in-law's defenders to his accusers, poignantly noting, "you die a little in the process." Robert Stevenson told me that it would have been "a lot easier for the family to believe someone else had done it."

Thus, Freddy and Mildred, for so long MacDonald's fervent champions, became his mortal enemies. Freddy was to be the lead

MAKING LAW

public avenger, and now would dedicate himself to an even more intense campaign to force the Army to prosecute the man whose innocence he and Mildred had previously proclaimed.

The Army's investigators in the CID had interviewed MacDonald and testified during the Article 32 proceeding; they had never believed MacDonald's story, and now privately welcomed the Kassabs' stunning reversal. With the impetus that Freddy's new campaign gave them, the CID pressed internally for the Army to reopen the case, and in December 1970, the Army agreed to do so, authorizing CID to conduct what became an 18-month reinvestigation.

The top brass had approved the reopening of the investigation with misgivings because the Army had legally lost jurisdiction over MacDonald when he was discharged, but the pressure for a reinvestigation was too strong to ignore.

In June 1972, the Army delivered to the Department of Justice a 3,000-page report of the reinvestigation, containing hundreds of exhibits. The CID findings made a strong circumstantial case against MacDonald.

If a prosecution were to take place then, the Department of Justice would have to authorize it. But time continued to pass after the report landed in Washington, and every day the Kassabs awaited some indication of the government's intentions, but there was none.

Deeply frustrated, Fred and Mildred turned to Richard Scheyer, a lawyer in Smithtown, Long Island, who had handled the sale of their house. Dick and I were licensed private pilots and had spent considerable time together taking turns flying a Piper Cherokee 6 seven-seat airplane to distant places with our families. We called the plane "Zero-Four Romeo;" its full identifier was N-4104-R.

Dick practiced law in the state courts, and because these murders took place on a military base, any prosecution would have to take place in the federal courts, where I regularly practiced. Dick referred the Kassabs to me, and thus in late 1972 began my involvement in the second triple murder case of my career, this time "unofficially," neither as prosecutor nor defense counsel. I was squarely on the side of whoever turned out to be MacDonald's prosecutor, if there was ever to be one.

Freddy was stocky and mostly bald, and when we met he would usually have a cigar between his teeth. There was something compelling about this man sitting across from me; at 51, he was aging a bit, but his body was strong and tense. The murders and the campaign he and Mildred were conducting had energized him with a kind of smoldering power. His mind was as retentive and responsive as that of a much younger man. The information he gave me was always clear, accurate, and reliable; although he expressed his views with great passion and colorful language, I never found him to exaggerate or embellish the facts. I thought of him not only as a man of courage, but as thoroughly honest and decent. But during that difficult period, he did not have many occasions to show me the "gentle" side of his personality that Bob Stevenson remembered.

When Freddy wished to vent, he did so very effectively; he could show disdain for the views of those who disagreed with him, but he would always back up that disdain with a pitch-perfect and precisely organized recital of the evidence and arguments supporting his claims.

Freddy's verbal clashes with the federal government became more strident. He was dismissive of normal social customs, once writing directly to the very federal judge whom with trepidation we had involved in the case. Those in power continued to resist prosecuting these crimes, and Freddy's combative instincts took control. He baited adversaries, sent numerous letters which he released to the press, and issued streams of *ad hominem* public statements which cut his antagonists to shreds.

I never questioned his right to do those less attractive things: an unspeakable tragedy had destroyed his family. I wished he had been more controllable, but there was no denying that his dynamism was effective: his unrelenting campaign to obtain justice, coupled with his colorful and confrontational personality, propelled the case into the public consciousness.

There was much more information that Freddy had to master in his second campaign than was necessary for the first, but he did it. He took care of the practical chores as well: having compiled contact information for all of the news organizations covering the matter, he was able, on several hours' notice, to summon key reporters of the *New York Times and Newsday*, the national news services, and the broadcast media, for one of his own numerous "press conferences." Just as Freddy had minced no words in proclaiming his son-in-law's innocence, he did the same in urging his prosecution.

Mildred's demeanor in our meetings contrasted sharply with Freddy's: he was inclined to be bombastic, but she was soft of speech to the point of sometimes being inaudible. But her quiet passion to see that the now-identified perpetrator was brought to justice was even more poignant, because she spoke so little. Her body, dainty and self-contained in repose, during some discussions became tense and rigid. One of the outward signs of her agitation was a cloud of cigarette smoke that sometimes obscured my view of her. She and Freddy agreed on much about the case, and communicated non-verbally, with a few sparse words or a glance. When his nasal voice began to rise and his gestures became more emphatic, he would often turn toward her, as if to reassure himself that she agreed with what he was saying. She would murmur one or two words or barely perceptibly nod her head. Each of them deeply cared about what the other was feeling.

Freddy confirmed this when he wrote about the terrible day they learned about the murders, and the Army flew them down to Ft. Bragg and put them up in the visiting generals' quarters: "Mildred and I couldn't sleep but stranger was that we didn't speak a word to each other. ... God knows there were a million things to say—but it was as if each of us was encased in a thick cover of numbness. Words couldn't go in or out. We both sensed what it was so there was no feeling of estrangement. We were together and close even if we couldn't say a word."

My first action on behalf of Fred and Mildred was to write a letter in mid-December 1972 to a man I still thought of as a friend: L. Patrick Gray, who had hired me 12 years before to work for "Citizens for Nixon" during Vice President Nixon's first presidential campaign in the summer of 1960. I liked Gray and saw him as a fair and decent man. He was now President Nixon's acting Director of the FBI, and I requested that the Bureau review the Army's files.

I was therefore disappointed to receive a formal response from the Bureau, dated January 4, 1973 and signed not by Gray but by one of his assistants, stating, "inasmuch as there was no evidence indicating civilian subjects were involved, the FBI had no jurisdiction." An unusual note attached to the FBI letter gave me some information I had not known about. It charged that "the investigation into the brutal slayings was mishandled by the Army from the outset" and that "initially the military refused to turn over evidence to the FBI."

I wasn't surprised to see the bitter inter-departmental resentments recorded on the paper in front of me, and wondered if the conflict was contributing to the government's inaction on the case.

MAKING LAW

I sent my letter at a very bad time for Pat Gray. Unbeknownst to me, the FBI was engaged in a frenzied attempt to get to the bottom of the Watergate break-in, and was collecting evidence that had begun to indicate that the Nixon White House, and possibly even the President, were involved. Without getting into the story of "Deep Throat," a/k/a Mark Felt, his assistant, Gray had immense problems on his plate, and whatever its reasons, the F.B.I. would not take any action in the MacDonald matter.

I no longer knew anybody to call at the Justice Department where I had worked 16 years before, but it was already clear to me that the Department, the FBI's parent agency, had no appetite to pursue a case against MacDonald. The Army wasn't empowered to act, and the civilian authorities in Justice were uninterested.

In "How It All Started," another of his unpublished essays, Freddy Kassab wrote about his "constant battle with the U.S. Department of Justice" from June 1972 on:

> The fight started with my first meeting in Raleigh, North Carolina with the then U.S. Attorney for that area, Warren Coolidge, and two of his assistant U.S. Attorneys. The meeting lasted all day. We went over the Army report. Coolidge stated to me at that time that he would only prosecute if he determined that there was at least an "80 percent probability" of his winning the case, and that he and he alone would decide; furthermore, his decision would be final. To emphasize this, he showed me a letter signed by six or seven assistant U.S. Attorneys in December of 1970 (right after MacDonald was discharged from the Army). The letter stated that since MacDonald was now a civilian and under their jurisdiction,

they wanted him prosecuted and threatened to resign if this was not done. He refused.

The trip was not totally useless: one of Coolidge's assistants was on my side and argued with me against his boss, but it did no good. On September 8, 1972, the day before his resignation as U.S. Attorney, Coolidge wrote a letter to the Attorney General in Washington declining to prosecute.

The battle royal then started in with Washington. The result was that the case was assigned to a group of lawyers in the Criminal Division. They had it from September of 1972 until March of 1973; nothing happened. Meanwhile, my lawyer and I were constantly on their back.

One of Coolidge's assistants was Thomas McNamara, who suddenly succeeded Coolidge as U.S. Attorney in September 1972, when Coolidge, for reasons unrelated to the MacDonald case, was summoned to Washington and ordered to resign.

As an Assistant U.S. Attorney, McNamara had long been interested in the MacDonald murders, and he had been concerned for some time about the lack of action. He was sworn in as the new U.S. Attorney, and shortly thereafter assigned the case to himself. Over the following months, he visited the still-sealed crime scene at Fort Bragg and made at least a half-dozen trips to Washington to try and persuade his Justice Department superiors—in particular, Carl Belcher, head of the General Crimes Section—to put the case before a grand jury. McNamara kept saying, "we can't sit on this case any longer," but Belcher would not move.

McNamara was determined to see if some critical but overlooked information was contained somewhere in the voluminous

MAKING LAW

files of the case he kept in his office. The product of his study was a 10-page memorandum outlining the evidence, which he completed and sent to Washington in June 1973. He was concerned about the government's inability to prove a motive but made no effort to conceal his opinion about who was responsible for the crimes: "I am convinced that Jeffrey MacDonald brutally murdered his wife and two children during the late evening and early morning hours of February 16-17, 1970. But I am afraid we will not be able to convict him." McNamara then commented, "I sincerely hope that when the Justice Department reevaluates this case, it will be given a better chance of success. I would like to see this murderer brought to trial." He then asked Washington to lend his office one of the Criminal Division's most experienced trial lawyers.

The Kassabs and I had never seen McNamara's recommendation, but knew that he believed that MacDonald was guilty. Freddy was constantly pressuring McNamara to take action, but McNamara didn't want to broadcast his frustrations with his superiors in Washington. Ultimately, he felt he had to tell Freddy that they had failed to give him the authority he needed to begin a prosecution.

In December 1973, the Kassabs' consternation deepened when an Assistant Attorney General wrote to tell them that the case had been referred back to the Army, a ridiculous and patently untrue statement; everyone knew that the Army no longer had jurisdiction.

There had never been any referral to the Army, and why the Kassabs were given totally false information was never explained, then or since.

Freddy's patience ran out. In a typically blistering letter (what the reporters had come to call "Freddy letters"), he demanded that the Army officially state its position.

Now, however, Freddy's urgent demand—which could have been quickly batted aside by the Army by simply writing back to say that they no longer had any authority to act in the case—produced a surprise. Three weeks after receiving Freddy's letter, Major Steven Chucala, the Staff Judge Advocate, wrote back and told him that "an exhaustive analysis of the facts and relevant law" led him to conclude that the reinvestigation had established "a prima facie case."

At no time before that had any responsible Army officer publicly expressed second thoughts about the decision in the Article 32 proceeding. Legally, the letter from Chucala was irrelevant because the Army had no jurisdiction over the matter. Armed with it, however, Freddy reached out to the members of the Judiciary Committee of the House of Representatives, but that effort merely provoked Belcher in January 1974 to write, "We have concluded that the evidence currently available is insufficient to warrant prosecution at this time."

I was encouraged by Major Chucala's words but frustrated that he technically had no clout in the matter. We had run out of conventional options. We had to devise some new strategy.

Captain Peter Kearns was the key CID investigator involved in the Army's reinvestigation. He was one of a small group of Army investigators, who, contrary to Col. Rock's findings, had no doubt from the outset about MacDonald's guilt. He had led the charge to conduct the reinvestigation and was the principal author of the reinvestigation report. Although I knew his bias, his personal knowledge of the evidence and his expertise as an investigator would be extremely helpful.

I called Kearns, and he verbally "walked me through" the evidence. I asked if he would come up to Long Island so I could put everything he was telling me in an affidavit. He told me he'd get back to me. I learned years later that he had immediately consulted with his friend Brian Murtagh, a 28-year-old Army JAG officer who was also working for Major Chucala in CID; the two

MAKING LAW

men had met in the CID office and bonded two years before, and Kearns had great respect for Murtagh's legal abilities. It would turn out that, except for trying the government's criminal case 16 years later against the two Libyans charged with bringing down Pan Am Flight 103, Murtagh went on to devote virtually his entire legal career to the MacDonald case.

Kearns had retired the year before our telephone conversation; he wanted to make an affidavit for us, but he was concerned what would happen if he did so. He decided to call Murtagh for advice at 2 a.m. the next morning. "I'm still a good cop," he said, "but will they take my pension if I do this?" Murtagh reassured him that that they could not do that; soon thereafter, Kearns was in my office in Huntington reciting the details of the case all over again.

His encyclopedic recall of the facts was so impressive that I asked Barbara Pedersen, my secretary, to take down his entire narrative in shorthand. What he told her was so horrifying that years later she still remembered vividly how difficult it had been for her to remain calm while she took down the gruesome details.

By the time Kearns and I met, it was late winter 1974, more than four years after the murders. I had been representing the Kassabs for nearly half of that time, and as my conviction about MacDonald's guilt grew, my doubts about the ultimate success of any criminal prosecution were growing. There were speedy trial rules and the crimes were fast receding into the past. By now, some witnesses' memories had undoubtedly faded. Further delay might doom an ultimate prosecution.

Private parties never play an official role in initiating a criminal prosecution. The decision whether or not to bring criminal charges against someone is always made by a government official: in federal cases, that official is usually the local United States Attorney. Prosecutors have virtually unlimited discretion whether or not to charge someone with a crime, and the courts had repeatedly made clear that they would not "interfere with prosecutorial discretion."

However, McNamara's memorandum, the Army's reinvestigation report and Maj. Chucala's recent letter, all concluding that a prima facie case existed, were unusual features in this case. Two high-ranking government lawyers and the Army's elite criminal investigators all stated in writing that they believed that MacDonald was guilty and should be prosecuted. The immediate problem was that McNamara, the local U.S. Attorney having direct jurisdiction of the case and convinced of MacDonald's guilt, had asked for authority to initiate a prosecution, but his superiors had refused to give it to him.

McNamara could be a strong ally, if he could be set free to express his views. I wanted to find a way to bring him into federal court so that, if the judge asked him, he would be compelled to truthfully disclose his professional judgment.

Rule 3 of the United States Rules of Criminal Procedure prescribed how a criminal prosecution was to be instituted. I read it carefully:

> Rule 3. The Complaint.
>
> The complaint is a written statement of the essential facts constituting the offense charged. It shall be made upon oath before a magistrate.

This very succinct rule became critical to our strategy not because of its content, but because of its omission. It did not require, on its face at least, that a criminal complaint be presented by a prosecutor; therefore, it was—at least theoretically—open for anyone to do so. But that kind of interpretation of the rule seemed inconsistent with the rule that gave nearly absolute "prosecutorial discretion" to U.S. Attorneys. I could find only two reported court cases in which citizens tried to institute criminal prosecutions, and they had both failed.

However, I felt that Rule 3 might force the government to publicly commit itself. If I drew up a criminal complaint and presented it to a judge in the Eastern District of North Carolina, where Fort Bragg was located, backed up by the Kassabs' testimony about the false accounts their son-in-law had given them and by a statement from Kearns, who was familiar with the evidence that contradicted MacDonald's account, and if all of that evidence pointed to MacDonald's probable guilt, perhaps the judge would think long and hard about how to handle the matter, and would almost certainly consult with U.S. Attorney McNamara. It might not work, but it was the only strategy we had.

I decided to present the case not to a magistrate, but rather to the highest-ranking judge in the eastern district of North Carolina. That was Chief Judge Algernon Butler, who was appointed by President Eisenhower fifteen years earlier; after only two years of service he had been elevated to Chief Judge. He was credited with desegregating the schools in the eastern part of North Carolina and was widely respected in legal circles for his ability and judgment. He was one of a small number of jurists that appear in each generation who deserved the highest accolade that his colleagues could confer upon him: he was a "judge's judge." He was exactly the kind of judge I hoped would hear the Kassabs' complaint.

I outlined the plan to Freddy and Mildred. We would present the papers to Chief Judge Butler, if he would see us. If he accepted our papers, he would be required to decide whether there is "probable cause to believe that an offense has been committed and that the defendant has committed it." If he determined that both answers were yes, he was required either to issue a warrant for the defendant's arrest or convene a grand jury. Whichever avenue the judge chose would provide some action in the case.

So, on April 22, 1974, having no idea what to expect, I telephoned Judge Butler's chambers. A startled judge came to the phone and listened. I explained that we had prepared a Rule 3 criminal complaint regarding the MacDonald murders, and wished to present it to him. I finished what I wanted to say, and waited for his reaction.

"Can you come down here to my chambers and see me next week?" he asked.

"Yes, Judge, we will be there."

We had taken the first step, and Butler hadn't rebuffed us. Now we had to prepare for the unknown—and get plane tickets.

I knew that Judge Butler would ask McNamara to be present when the Kassabs and I appeared in his chambers. He would then inform his superiors in the Justice Department in Washington—and they would not be pleased.

The Justice Department would have at least three options: their lawyers could travel to North Carolina and preempt McNamara; they could allow McNamara to appear as a free agent; or they could file papers in an attempt to dissuade Butler from seeing us. I could not predict what the lawyers in my old building in Washington, or Judge Butler, would do.

I learned afterwards that the Kassabs and I were not the only people who were uncertain how the scenario would play out. The key officials of the Justice Department—in particular Carl Belcher, to whom McNamara had addressed his prosecutorial memorandum—had long ago made up their minds not to authorize a prosecution, and nothing in the law required them to change their position. There was a high likelihood that Belcher would prod his superiors to ask Judge Butler to rule that we had no right to intrude upon the government's discretionary decisions. But, such a scenario carried its risks: the Justice Department's position would

MAKING LAW

immediately be publicized, if not by the Court, then surely by Freddy Kassab. If Justice's lawyers stuck to their guns, they almost certainly would have to publicly explain at some point why they were unwilling to have a grand jury hear evidence of indisputably horrendous crimes, and the public might not react well.

The public official in the center of this developing drama, Judge Butler, had never been faced by this situation before, and was uncertain what he should do; private citizens, as contrasted with a government prosecutor, would in several days be in his chambers to present a criminal complaint to him. Immediately after my call, he discussed the matter extensively with McNamara and two days later with Weldon Hollowell, for some years a well-respected assistant U.S. Attorney in the district. McNamara's office plunged into legal research and McNamara shared what little they found with the judge. There was not a lot of case authority to guide any of us.

We had given Judge Butler a difficult problem and had also placed McNamara in an uncomfortable position because of the conflict between his personal views and those of his Justice Department superiors.

The situation could end up in a "no win" situation for McNamara, or for Washington—or both. If McNamara encouraged Butler to act on our request, the Justice Department's long-standing opposition to a prosecution would be effectively undercut by its own representative; but even if the Judge followed McNamara's lead, vindictive bureaucrats at Justice might later find a way to cut short McNamara's government career.

I thought we were taking a necessary step that might advance the Kassabs' quest. McNamara had a duty as a lawyer to be candid with the judge, and I had a feeling that he would honor that duty. I thought the odds were in our favor that McNamara would reaffirm his belief in MacDonald's guilt and his opinion that he should be prosecuted.

After my call, McNamara wrote to the judge and stated the Justice Department's official position, that there was not "sufficient evidence to obtain a conviction of Dr. MacDonald." Then he immediately wrote another letter, stating his own view: "I guess you can entertain Mr. Kahn's (sic) private citizen's complaint but hopefully in your discretion, you will deny the issuance of an arrest warrant." I didn't mind that he had misspelled my name and had opposed an arrest warrant; he had left wide open the possibility that Judge Butler could convene a grand jury.

Freddy, Mildred and I flew to Raleigh, North Carolina, on April 30, and were met by Kearns, who drove us to the post office building in Clinton, 70 miles away, where Judge Butler had his chambers. I knew nothing yet about any communications between McNamara and the judge. I was carrying three legal documents I had prepared back at my office in Huntington, and some optimism, that I hoped would survive the morning.

Shortly after 10:30 a.m., we all entered Judge Butler's chambers. Algernon Butler was 69 years old. He wore rimless glasses; a wisp of white hair was barely visible above his large forehead. He was a bit formal but rose from his chair and extended his hand to each of us, and smiled. We also shook hands with Tom McNamara, the United States Attorney, now standing at the side of the Judge's desk, with whom Freddy had spent considerable time, and also with Christine Witcover, one of McNamara's Assistant U.S. Attorneys. McNamara mentioned that he had grown up on Long Island, and I wondered whether his special interest in the case might have been triggered by the fact that all the principals in this case—MacDonald, Freddy, Mildred, and Colette—had also lived there for many years. Years later, McNamara told me that there were two other things that had motivated him the day we met in Judge Butler's chambers: the horrifying facts of the case themselves, and Freddy Kassab's single-minded quest for justice. I

MAKING LAW

came to believe that the more resistance McNamara encountered from his superiors in Washington to convene a grand jury investigation, the more determined he also had become. He was a principled and dedicated lawyer, a credit to our profession, and I admire him for that. It was no surprise to me to learn, when I contacted him in recent years about this book, that he was still serving the justice system, as the Chief Public Defender in the Eastern District of North Carolina.

I thanked Judge Butler for entertaining our application and he invited me to speak. With an unsteady voice I began with a description of the crime scene encountered by the Army MPs on that fatal night, where the victims were found, and the injuries inflicted upon their bodies. I did not need to use many adjectives to convey the horror of the scene, and my emotions were close to the surface. Everyone present knew that these unprecedented proceedings in Judge Butler's chambers were necessitated by the most egregious of events. Except for the sound of my voice, the room was silent.

I summarized the odd history of the case: starting with the Article 32 proceeding and ending with Maj. Chucala's bombshell letter stating that, contrary to the Army's prior conclusion, the evidence showed that a case existed. Judge Butler was taking detailed notes on a long legal pad.

The Rule 3 Complaint laid out what Mildred and Freddy knew, and Peter Kearns' affidavit described what the reinvestigation that he led, had found; the judge had not had a chance to read them, so I laid out the important parts of the evidence. I wasn't a neutral observer, but I knew to a certainty that our papers showed more than enough to justify prosecution. I just didn't know if the judge would feel he had the authority to act upon them.

I did take several minutes to dwell on the shocking information that MacDonald had placed in his father-in-law's hands. Nine months after the murders, MacDonald called Freddy and told him he had "gone hunting" for the murderers of his family and had found a suspect. He said he had beaten and questioned the man, who finally admitted to participating in the murders. MacDonald said that he had then killed him. Immediately after that telephone call, he sent a note to Freddy, saying, "I will deny our phone conversation of today if anyone ever asks. I am sure you can figure out why. What must be done must be done."

There was only one homicide during that period, the victim being an Army sergeant with no connection to the MacDonald killings, shot five times in the back. At his trial five years later, MacDonald finally admitted on the witness stand that he had made up "a lie of incredible proportions."

McNamara sat quietly during my presentation. When I finished, Judge Butler asked him to state his position. He confirmed that his earlier memorandum had recommended prosecution and that his recommendation had been rejected by the Justice Department. Then McNamara looked directly at the Judge, paused a moment, and said the words I had long hoped he would say: "I am not a free agent. My hands are tied."

I shifted my gaze from McNamara to the Judge. I did not know to what extent the two men had discussed the case, but I had the sense that McNamara was telling Judge Butler what the judge already knew. I also had the impression that this judge, as careful as he was to conceal his opinion from us, shared McNamara's views. I thought then, and think now, that he welcomed an opportunity to force Washington to act in the case.

After McNamara spoke, I felt I had to say something about the conflict between McNamara and the Justice Department. "If the Justice Department instructs Mr. McNamara not to sign an indictment, or prosecute, then I recognize how tempting it will be for the Court to deny our application," I said. "After all, it would be very time-consuming and a waste of everybody's money to do so since a prosecution cannot thereafter proceed without the government's commitment to pursue it. But we respectfully submit that that would be wrong; even if the procedure ultimately turns out to be futile, we urge the Court to follow it, because, in fairness, in light of the evidence, the atrocity of these crimes, and the fact that they occurred on a government reservation, if the government declines to pursue this case, at least it should be compelled to explain why."

The judge gave no outward indication of his feelings. He stood up, and asked Fred, Mildred, and Peter also to stand and raise their right hands. They did, and all swore to the truth of the statements in the legal papers. McNamara's Assistant looked on quietly. McNamara was quiet but there was a slight smile of satisfaction on his face.

We had spent less than an hour in Judge Butler's chambers, and as we prepared to leave, the momentousness of what we were doing sank in. All four of us had the sense that this odd ceremony we had just participated in would set something in motion—we did not know exactly what—but it would significantly change the outcome of this drama.

Judge Butler thanked us for coming and then turned to me to say that he had not yet decided whether to "accept" the complaint as an official court filing. Words automatically came out of my mouth: "Thank you, Judge, I understand," although I didn't.

When I initially thought about it, I chalked it up to the Judge's uncertainty about what procedure he should follow, but I now believe he had a plan very much in mind: by not accepting the papers as an "official" filing, he escaped the strictures of Federal Rule 4, which would have forced *him* to make a preliminary decision on MacDonald's probable guilt. I am now sure Butler believed that it was inappropriate for him to make that decision, and that he—and the public—needed the government to make it. He purposely kept the government guessing about his intentions, figuring that an implicit threat to "officially" file our papers might be a more potent way of persuading the government to act than actually filing them.

Despite that odd caveat, I felt a sense of satisfaction. However, as we were walking toward the door, Judge Butler had another surprise: he was going to the hospital the next day to have his pacemaker replaced, and he'd address our papers when he got back. "O, my God," I thought to myself, "what if Judge Butler dies, and we have to do this all over again?"

After we left, McNamara again discussed the case with Judge Butler. Butler was deeply troubled by the case, and, like McNamara, felt it should be brought to a public conclusion one way or the other. He asked McNamara to make one more visit to his superiors in Washington and, in light of our presentation, see if they still were unwilling to present the case to a grand jury. McNamara agreed. He was not optimistic that anything would change, but it did.

Back in New York some months later, I was told by Bob Keeler, a Newsday reporter who covered the MacDonald case extensively, that after our appearance, Judge Butler telephoned Attorney General William Saxbe and asked him to have a Justice Department representative appear at his courtroom in North Carolina and explain why the government would not issue an arrest warrant for MacDonald. That generally described Judge Butler's intentions, but it was wrong in the details: Judge Butler had not waited until after his pacemaker replacement to take action, and he didn't make a phone call; on the morning of May 1st, just before he went for his procedure, he put four questions to the government in writing. "Dear Mr. Attorney General," he said, "please advise me with respect to the following:

1. Will the United States attorney prepare and submit a signed indictment to a grand jury charging the defendant with the three alleged capital felonies?
2. If the grand jury should return a true bill of indictment, will the United States prosecute the case?
3. If a grand jury should be convened to hear the evidence in this case, would the United States attorney cooperate with the grand jury in its investigation and draft indictments, if any, in accordance with its desires and sign any indictment that may be found by the grand jury?
4. If the United States attorney should decline to sign an indictment, or if the government should decline to prosecute, please disclose fully the government's reason for its decisions."

I have kept a framed copy of this extraordinary letter for more than 40 years.

The Judge returned from the hospital, but there was no word from Saxbe; so, on June 14th, he wrote again, more pointedly telling the Attorney General: "I will appreciate a reply." Butler was determined to force the government to take a position, McNamara had made yet another visit to Washington, but the Justice Department lawyers did not want to answer the judge's letter at all.

Assistant Attorney General Henry Petersen was Belcher's supervisor, and he took action. Overruling Belcher, he advised Butler that he had assigned the matter to Victor Worheide, one of his "most skilled trial attorneys," that Worheide would review the file, and that the government would present the case to a grand jury if he concluded that the case would survive a motion to dismiss at the close of the prosecution's case. McNamara remembered Worheide as "on in years [he was 64], and a bit grouchy," but "a tireless, dogged prosecutor" with an excellent track record, who for years had been sent all over the country by the Justice Department to try difficult cases.

Murtagh had been introduced to the MacDonald case from the moment he had joined CID two years before. He knew Worheide's reputation, and when he learned that he had been tasked with presenting the case to a grand jury, the 28-year-old Murtagh telephoned him "with trepidation;" he wanted to be involved in the case. Then, when Worheide answered, his voice came through "like a foghorn—it made walls shake." Not knowing what else to say, or how Worheide would respond, he offered to drive the older man to CID headquarters to show him the files.

"Meet me at 10th and Constitution in 10 minutes," Worheide said loudly, and shortly thereafter Murtagh spotted an elderly, hulking figure, wearing a red tie, straw homburg hat, with cigar ashes trailing down the front of his suit. On that day, the rest of Murtagh's professional career was written.

Freddy, Mildred and I did not know that McNamara was going to Washington again. By June 30th, Freddy was completely frustrated, and without advising me what he was doing, he wrote a "Freddy letter" to Judge Butler. I was distraught that he had done so and now I was concerned that his letter might derail whatever plan Butler was following. Freddy at least had let me off the hook by saying, "I was told by my attorney that one does not write letters to judges." He expressed his "contempt" for the Justice Department and bemoaned the fact that he and Mildred didn't "have the means to hire high-powered and high-pressure attorneys" but "we do have the determination to see to it that the murderer of our daughter and two granddaughters is brought to justice." When I saw Freddy's comments about not being able to hire high-powered lawyers, I didn't know whether I should be flattered or insulted.

Judge Butler had kept the pressure on Saxbe and Petersen, and they sent Worheide to North Carolina to meet with him.

MAKING LAW

Worheide, a grandfather himself, had taken one look at the crime scene photographs of the two dead children and was ready to take the case on.

As soon as Worheide left, Butler began to make the necessary arrangements to convene a grand jury.

Then, in another act of monumental misjudgment, MacDonald elected to testify before the grand jury and made several more statements about the events of February 17 that conflicted with the known evidence.

In January 1975, the grand jury indicted him for the three killings, and the FBI arrested him.

Four years of legal maneuvering followed before the trial finally began, in July 1979. I flew to Raleigh to hear MacDonald testify. I had never seen the man about whom I had written so much.

The photographs I had seen and the descriptions I had heard (even from Freddy and Mildred) made clear that MacDonald had been an attractive, rather tall and lean young man. Now, nine years after the start of the long, convoluted legal proceedings, his hair was graying, and he was showing his weight. It was hard to identify the man I watched on the witness stand with those old photographs.

MacDonald showed little emotion. By then, that was no surprise to any of us. On the Dick Cavett show before a nationwide TV audience in December 1970, he was asked about the murders of his family only ten months before, and, as Bob Stevenson said, "all he could talk about was how his rights had been violated. I don't think he once said, let's get the murderers. He was grinning like a Cheshire cat." Cavett himself, an experienced interviewer, was in disbelief: "Jeez, you find your wife and kid have been murdered, and his answer about that was, 'Hey,' and he says something that sounded like Bob Hope? ... His affect was wrong, completely wrong."

It seemed impossible that this controlled, emotionless witness had ever grieved the loss of the wife and two children he professed to have loved. Sitting at the trial, I remembered Freddy telling me that he had learned that only three or four nights after the murders, MacDonald had his friends bring a bottle of champagne and a bottle of whiskey to his hospital room and they all had a party. From what I saw of MacDonald at the trial, I believed it.

I was sorry I did not hear the closing argument by Assistant U.S. Attorney Jim Blackburn. In a brilliant and incisive moment, he suggested that Colette's purported cry that MacDonald claimed to have heard, "Jeff, why are they doing this to me?"—a highly improbable statement that a woman under mortal attack would make—had been critically edited by MacDonald, and that what she had almost certainly said was "Jeff, why are *you* doing this to me?" Freddy, who was present in the courtroom, felt that in that one electrifying comment, Blackburn had supplied the jurors and the spectators with the missing key to the case: a condemnation of the defendant by his deceased victim, in her own words.

On August 30th, I was working at my office. The phone rang, Vivian was on the line; she had been listening to the radio, waiting for the verdict. We had the shortest conversation she and I ever had.

"Guilty," she said.

"Hard to believe," I said.

MacDonald was sentenced to three consecutive life terms. His application in 2005 for parole was denied, and as of this writing, he remains in prison.

Judge Butler died in September, 1978, about four and a half years after we had seen him, and a year before the final verdict. He had never lived to see the trial that had resulted from his unconventional intervention in the case. He was rightfully proud of his role in this drama; among the documents that he donated to the library of the University of North Carolina at Chapel Hill were his papers relating to this case, including his handwritten notes of our 1974 meeting in his chambers in the lower floor of the post office in Clinton.

The application that the Kassabs and I made to Judge Butler received remarkably careful judging. Although no one to my knowledge had ever gone so far as to present a formal Rule 3 complaint to a federal judge, and there was no precedent directing him to reject ours, Butler could easily have refused to meet with us, telling us that nothing could be accomplished by such a meeting, because federal and state prosecutors alone had the discretion to bring or decline to prosecute criminal charges in a particular case.

I did not immediately appreciate the delicate and deliberate process adopted by Butler. He never ruled on the validity of our Rule 3 complaint, and in the end neither accepted nor rejected it. He never placed himself in a position where he had to decide whether private citizens had legal standing to file a criminal complaint in the absence of a decision by the prosecutors whether or not to prosecute. His touch was so light, that without committing himself to a legal position he allowed the circumstances created by our presentation to force the prosecutors themselves to make a definitive prosecutorial decision. The public interest was well served by his strategy: even if the Justice Department had stuck to its prior refusal to prosecute, the public would at least know why.

Even though he did something extraordinary, he did it without undermining long-settled precedent forbidding judges from interfering with the Department's discretion; in fact, he reinforced it. He achieved justice by keeping that precedent as a non-issue in the case, by brilliantly disguising a meaningful decision as a non-decision.

So, many years later, as I read his handwritten notes for the first time, I thought of the elderly, ailing Judge Butler, just as much a stranger to the unprecedented procedure as I was, carefully thinking out what his duty required him to do at every step of the way. And doing it perfectly.

Former U.S. Attorney Thomas McNamara, whose personal and professional view of what should be done clashed with the wishes of his superiors in Washington; and who as a result must have experienced considerable personal anguish, did what he felt he had to do, by disclosing the internal Justice Department conflict and candidly advising Judge Butler what he thought should be done in the case. Had he played his role differently, it is unclear how this story would have ended.

Our family's involvement in the case came to a close when NBC released the made-for-TV movie based upon Joe McGinnis' book *"Fatal Vision."* In a key scene, crafted with more than a bit of artistic license, the actor Karl Malden, playing Fred Kassab, is seen poring over books in a law library, and finds something useful in one of the court decisions he is researching. He looks up and says to his wife, "Mildred, do you remember that lawyer Cahn who told us we could file our own criminal complaint against Jeff?" That's when my children got the idea for the key chain with "Lawyer Cahn" engraved on it; and that's what they called me for quite a while afterward.

8

DID A COMPUTER SYSTEM NAMED MERS DESTROY THE WORLD ECONOMY?

After the world's financial system collapsed in 2007, I saw only a few references to "MERS," short for "Mortgage Electronic Recording System." I was surprised about that, because I believed it played a huge role in bringing about that debacle.

The more I thought about the lawsuit that MERS won against Edward Romaine, Suffolk's County Clerk, the more I wondered whether the financial disaster would have occurred at all if that case had come out the other way. I knew about that strange case of MERS v Romaine, because I was Romaine's lawyer. It masqueraded as a case about the technical requirements of mortgage instruments and ended with a pronouncement from New York's highest judges that they didn't care about those requirements at the moment. But it was a far, far more important case than they, or anyone else, realized then.

Before I tell you about that, let me take you to 2007.

That was when a very exciting financial ride enjoyed by many came to an end. In the red-hot real estate market leading up to that year, you could buy a house almost anywhere, "flip" it quickly, and pocket a hefty profit. It was even sweeter if you bought it with borrowed money, because you had "leverage," and selling it in a rising market would bring you a much higher return on your investment than if you had paid all cash for it, and a lot of people were taking advantage of that economic law.

Borrowed money flooded the market. Far too much of it was in circulation, and true to the laws of supply and demand, it was sucked up by, and contributed to, a much too rapid rise in house prices all over the country. Homes were being bought and sold at prices far in excess of their reasonable values. It was only a matter of time before prices would crash, and when they did, many homes were "underwater," worth less than what was owed on their mortgages. Their owners saw no point in continuing to make mortgage payments, and three million homes fell into foreclosure. Non-productive mortgages are not worth much, and a lot of people and institutions across the globe who had indirectly invested in them through a variety of recently invented and difficult to understand financial instruments saw them plummet in value too. There was another important part of the story, involving sub-prime mortgages, but I'll explain that later. A great many people, corporations, banks, pension funds, and the countries in which they did business, were badly hurt by the collapse of those "mortgage-backed" investments. That, without the gory details, was what happened in 2007.

But six years before, no one foresaw what was going to happen.

In May 2001, our County Executive, Robert Gaffney, asked me to represent Romaine, who had just been sued by a mysterious corporation that I had never heard of before. The facts seemed clear, and did not remotely seem to have anything to do with the securities markets.

By means of that lawsuit, MERS launched a single-minded campaign to prevent Romaine from doing his job in the way he and his counterparts everywhere in the English-speaking world had done for hundreds of years. But there was no obvious reason why that corporation and its backers were doing so.

By law, a county clerk (in some places, a "registrar") is the custodian of the records that show who owns or has a lien—typically a mortgage—upon any piece of real estate in the County. Romaine had refused to record several mortgages prepared by MERS, that he and the County's Official Examiner of Title, a detail-oriented lawyer named John Kennedy, felt were "very peculiar." MERS was determined to force him to mend his ways.

I looked at the instruments at issue, and had no question that Romaine and Kennedy were right. The documents were labelled "MORTGAGE," all right, but the language in them was unorthodox, self-contradictory, and incomprehensible even to the most experienced of real estate lawyers.

The documents Romaine rejected described "MERS" as the "mortgagee" of the property. For hundreds of years, that term was universally understood to refer to a lender, typically a bank, that acquired a property interest in real estate which would serve as security for the payment of a loan it made to the property owner. If the loan fell into default, the mortgagee could foreclose upon the property and take it away from the owner. However, the mortgages that caught Romaine's eye stated that MERS would have no interest in that property at all, and was to be deemed the "mortgagee for purposes of recording only." There was no way to ignore that contradiction: the document went out of its way to deny that MERS had any interest in the property while insisting that it be indexed in the County's official land records as having one.

Others shared Romaine and Kennedy's opinion. Even before Romaine was served with legal papers, county clerks in more than a dozen other New York counties were burning up the telephone wires talking to one another about MERS mortgages that they, too, had been asked to record. Their concerns came to the attention of the New York Attorney General, who issued an opinion advising the clerks to record the mortgages under the name of the actual mortgagee, not under MERS' name. As far as the AG was concerned, the document made it clear that MERS could not properly be called a "mortgagee" in the transaction. MERS later said that it had not been afforded the opportunity before the AG released his opinion to persuade him that he was wrong.

We didn't think the AG was wrong; to put it plainly, MERS was asking Romaine and his fellow clerks to record documents that misrepresented the nature of the real property interest involved, and the AG told the county clerks how to cure that misrepresentation.

The battle in which Romaine found himself turned out to be really with Fannie Mae, Freddie Mac, and some of the largest investment banks in the world. "Fannie" and "Freddie" were known as "Government-Sponsored Enterprises," although they were actually privately-owned. They had been created by Congress for the purpose of increasing the availability of mortgage money to help Americans own a home of their own. Fannie and Freddie insisted that more people would be able to acquire their own homes if MERS's system kept track of the successive owners of residential mortgages in America, instead of public offices like Romaine's doing so.

Many of the mortgages that Fannie and Freddie urgently wanted to be in the MERS system were destined to crash, but no one yet knew it.

Suffolk County Supreme Court Justice James Catterson, the first judge to hear the Romaine case, was as incredulous about those strange "mortgages" as Romaine and I had been. In our initial court appearance before him, he did not understand what was meant by "mortgagee for recording purposes only," and he repeatedly asked Charles ("Charlie") Martorana, MERS' lawyer, to explain "how is your client's company a mortgagee?" Thirty

MAKING LAW

pages of court proceedings followed, but Catterson, frustrated, finally told Martorana, "You can point to no single case in the State of New York which will allow your instruments to be recorded." The concerns of Romaine and his fellow county clerks about those documents were validated by Catterson, but, surprisingly, he was the only judge hearing the case during its voyage through the court system who at any point focused on the inconsistent language in the MERS mortgages. After hearing Martorana's plea that first day in court, he flatly refused to order Romaine to accept them. Unfortunately for Romaine's side of the case, MERS immediately appealed and, even though one justice expressed reservations, the appeals judges in Brooklyn overruled Catterson and ordered Romaine to record the mortgages until the case came to an end.

I had no doubt that Catterson's instinct was right. MERS was not providing any explanation for the peculiar wording in its documents that made any sense to Romaine, Kennedy, the New York Attorney General, Catterson or me. But the Appellate Division had now directed otherwise. Depositions and document discovery would now occupy most of my time.

Seeing the MERS documents and listening to witnesses' shifting explanations was a jarring experience. At first, MERS claimed that mortgages controlled by MERS through its system would be able to be transferred at any time without anyone being required to prepare "assignments," separate paper documents traditionally used to transfer a mortgage from one owner to another. When they were signed, they were placed in the public records for all to see. It was hard to believe MERS's original explanation, that its private "electronic recording system" was designed to avoid the $19 charge that Suffolk imposed for the recording of mortgage assignments, or that Fannie, Freddie, and the Mortgage Bankers of America (which also entered the case) felt so strongly about that small charge that they were willing to undertake what must have been monumental litigation expenses in order to change it; and sure enough, their explanation soon changed.

MERS then said that its system was needed to vastly speed up the process of re-circulating millions of dollars in mortgage funds, as transfers could be made with a click of a computer mouse. MERS had a website that boasted it had registered 50 million such mortgages nationwide in its system, and its mission was "to register every mortgage loan in the United States on the MERS System."

But fulfillment of that mission was going to create trouble for a lot of people: MERS's new form of mortgage instrument made it impossible to obtain current information from the public records. MERS wanted the public records to show MERS as "mortgagee" no matter who might come to own a mortgage after it was first recorded. The name of the party who actually owned it would only be available on MERS's computer system, to which the public would have no access. MERS's lawyers tried hard to avoid using the word, but their client was privatizing a record-keeping system that had been open to the public for more than two hundred years.

Even a homeowner would not know who held the mortgage on his home, and if he fell behind in his payments, he would not know who to negotiate with to try to readjust the terms of his loan. If he paid it off and MERS signed the "satisfaction" of the mortgage, he would have no way of knowing whether MERS was its real owner and had the authority to do so. When I asked Mark Fleming, an officer of Freddie Mac, in his deposition whether a member of the general public had access to the MERS database, he answered, "Absolutely not."

R.K. Arnold, a wiry Texas lawyer, was President of MERS. He looked and sounded like Ross Perot, had a southwestern twang and loved to talk a lot, and fast. When I took his deposition, rather than directly answer my questions, he preferred to give vivid descriptions of MERS' accomplishments: "Millions of Americans that have invested in the American housing industry, because, as you may know, Fannie and Freddie securities are held by virtually every 401k in the United States, and it is far and away the most solid investment on the globe".

His comments were puzzling to me, because they were not responsive to my questions, and did not seem to be pertinent to the legal case that I thought we were involved in.

It clearly excited Arnold that mortgages would be offered to "millions of Americans." He focused on the "money providers," and waving his arms for emphasis, he declared that "it has to do with the velocity, the liquidity of the money," which "shoots back down to the mortgage company, which can then loan the money again to a new consumer."

We understood that listing MERS as the owner was intended to make it possible to transfer ownership of mortgages without tracking down the actual owner for a signature; MERS would be a "stand-in" for that owner. The problem we saw was damage to the public records: no matter how many transfers of an instrument took place in the blink of a computer's eye, the County Clerk's record that the public could see would never change. That record at the beginning and the end of the process would still show MERS as the "mortgagee," even though the language of the instrument said it wasn't. Nine years later, the University of Cincinnati Law Review would publish an article entitled "Foreclosure, Subprime Mortgage Lending, and the Mortgage Electronic Recording System" which set forth many of the same arguments that we raised in the Romaine case, collecting them under the heading, "The Questionable Legal Foundation of MERS."

MERS insisted that its mortgages were legal, and that they were necessary. Charlie Martorana, its attorney, in that lengthy first court appearance before Judge Catterson, made it clear that mortgages with the language Romaine objected to were critical to the generation of funds on the scale that Arnold would later describe:

> Fannie Mae, Freddie Mac, major institutions ... are arranging for the sale and purchase of millions of dollars of mortgage-backed securities in this country, it's interstate commerce, it's the life blood of securities industries, *all founded on this little note and mortgage* (italics mine).

As implied by Martorana's statement, MERS's business plan would involve an overwhelming number of mortgage transfers, and would also directly depend upon its ability to strip from the public records the name of each new owner. MERS's founders had needed to be sure that they could sidestep the public records whenever a transfer took place, and sought a written opinion from Covington & Burling, one of the nation's most prestigious law firms, blessing the proposed procedure. When a copy of the Covington opinion was delivered to my office during document discovery, I was shocked to see its conclusion: "the public has no significant interest in learning the true identity" of the owner of any mortgage. Romaine could not have disagreed more.

In 2007, barely six months after the Court of Appeals rendered its decision in the Romaine case, the overheated real estate market began to totter and soon crashed, and with the collapse in value of mortgaged homes came a collapse in value of their mortgages. Financial institutions, pension funds, and large and small investors worldwide who had eagerly purchased "mortgage-backed securities" and other complicated investment vehicles, discovered that the value of those holdings had dropped with sickening speed, although they were backed by large bundles of mortgages on residential homes located in all parts of America. The theory had been that those securities were, as R.K. Arnold had described, "the safest investments on the planet," because it was thought to be highly unlikely that mortgages from so many different parts of the country would all go bad at the same time.

Apart from the overpriced real estate market, another important factor in the crash was the existence of a large number of "subprime" or "predatory" mortgages that had been issued to risky borrowers, often with hidden, substantial future costs to the borrower, and that had also been massively assembled into bundles supporting mortgage-backed securities. Because borrowers taking those mortgages started out with limited resources with which to make mortgage payments during the initial period, higher default rates would have been expected even without the significant jump in the interest rate that kicked in, sometimes in as little as two years after the issuance of an original mortgage. That dramatic rate increase undoubtedly pushed vast additional numbers of subprime borrowers into default. As of 2010, 25% of all subprime mortgages were delinquent, and between 40% and 50% of all subprime mortgages originated after 2006 were predicted to eventually end in foreclosure. Those precarious mortgages were the backup for large numbers of mortgage-backed securities. It was reported that MERS was a party to more subprime mortgage loans than any other.

Through mortgage-backed securities and other newly-crafted securities with dizzying acronyms, one-third of all American mortgages were held indirectly by European and American investors. Victims of the crash included three large British banks, Germany's two largest banks, and one bank in France; those six institutions alone reported a total of $162 billion in what they called "toxic assets" on their books. No major financial institution in America was left unscathed: Morgan Stanley, HSBC Bank, Bear Stearns, Lehman Brothers, J. P. Morgan Chase and Wachovia Bank, to name a few. Lehman, a solid institution founded in the 1800s, was allowed to perish. Bear Stearns and Merrill Lynch were gobbled up by other firms. American International Group, the largest insurer in the world, had made possibly the worst bet of its existence, on the presumed safety of these investments, and ended up needing—and taking—by some accounts, as much as $182 billion in bailouts from the U.S. Government.

The crash of 2007 instantly changed the Wall Street landscape. Banks overseas lost billions and took their nations' economies down with them. Virtually every country in Europe, including Ireland, known for nearly a decade as the "Celtic Tiger," fell into desperate recession, with unemployment soaring. In America, the number of unemployed reached 25 million. As 2008 arrived, the world looked very much like 1929.

The Romaine case was filed in 2001, unfolded and, by an accident of timing finally ended in December 2006, shortly before the first rumblings of the impending crash. No one during the time the case was pending saw disaster on the horizon. Romaine and I were keeping our focus on preserving the transparency of Suffolk County's records, dismissing Arnold's rapturous descriptions of the "velocity" of the money as nothing more than empty boasting, and irrelevant to the issues in the case.

The Mortgage Bankers Association fought us with passion, and clearly hated the idea that a mere County Clerk could derail their grand plan, whatever it was. They touted their knowledge, experience and expertise, wrapped themselves in the American flag, and told the courts that the MERS system was an integral part of their industry that would "ensure continued strength of the nation's residential, multinational and commercial real estate markets; extend access to affordable housing to all Americans and expand the availability of financing".

That system, they claimed, "facilitates the continuous flow of money" from the mortgage industry into the real estate markets. And they, like Arnold, spoke proudly of the "speed at which mortgages are sold in the mortgage markets." The absence of ever more mortgage money, they predicted, would cause property values to drop precipitously "because capital will dry up."

I remarked at the time that it sounded suspiciously like a description of a Ponzi scheme. But I didn't know how the pieces fit together.

Officers of Fannie and Freddie testified how the two corporations began to purchase loans and "provide liquidity by packaging the lenders' loans into mortgage-backed securities which can then be sold to investors in the national and international securities markets." They said that allowing Romaine to preserve the traditional public recording system would "disrupt the mortgage market" and significantly "increase costs for the American homeowner."

As the case came to an end in the lower court, Judge Catterson was hemmed in by the Appellate Division interim decision of 2001 that had required Romaine to record MERS mortgages while the case was in progress. Deciding final motions for judgment by both sides, Catterson ultimately directed him to record MERS mortgages, but found MERS's arguments regarding the recording of "satisfaction" or "discharge" instruments unpersuasive, and refused to order Romaine to record them. On the new appeal that followed, the Appellate Division again disagreed with him, and required Romaine to record both mortgages and discharges.

We received a welcome emotional lift when the Court of Appeals—which was not legally required to hear our appeal—issued a rare order granting our request to do so, and we soon faced stepped-up rhetoric, claiming that Romaine's rejection of any of the MERS documents "would unravel the practical business benefits provided by MERS" and "undermine federal housing policy." After all, MERS said, its procedures "only enhance the accuracy of land records without any negative effect on the rights of any parties." How wrong that turned out to be!

The Court of Appeals heard the case in late 2006, shortly before the vaunted "continued strength" of the mortgage markets began to look like a chimera; in short order after that, the "liquidity" that Fannie and Freddie boasted they were providing disappeared, the information available about mortgages was often neither current nor accurate, and the mortgage-backed investments about which Arnold had rhapsodized turned out to be something other than "the most solid investment on the globe."

In September 2008, I was not sorry to see the government takeover of Fannie and Freddie, our archenemies in the MERS suit. They had proved to be as hollow as the representations they had made to the Court.

I had argued that the MERS system was deceptive and dangerous to present and prospective property owners. Another lawyer entered the case and highlighted another destructive potential of the MERS system: to the rights of consumers.

April Charney, attorney for the Jacksonville Florida Legal Aid Society, submitted a potent "friend of the court" brief supporting us, on behalf of her organization and 10 other not-for-profits which advocated for the poor and helpless. She pointed out that consumer rights, particularly of the elderly and the poor, were being prejudiced by the MERS system, describing "millions of homeowners" encountering a "virtual black hole of information."

That was the preamble to the most important part of Charney's amicus brief. The federal government and New York State (among others), had passed laws outlawing "predatory" or "subprime" mortgages and giving victims of deceptive lending practices the right to sue not only the original bank and mortgage broker who had engaged in those practices, but also all later owners of the mortgage. Since under MERS's system, the identity of owners subsequent to the original mortgage transaction could not easily be discovered, MERS had erected an almost insurmountable barrier preventing victimized homeowners from protecting their rights. That argument caught the Court's attention.

Even before the Romaine case was over, the strange provisions in the original mortgages and the secrecy of the MERS records often combined to make it impossible even for the lawyers who were foreclosing on defaulted MERS mortgages to know who their client was. Court decisions in at least six states rejected MERS' claims that it owned the mortgages that its lawyers were trying to foreclose.

By the time the Court of Appeals heard the case, courts in New York, Connecticut, Massachusetts, Georgia, Nebraska and Florida, had dismissed foreclosure actions brought by MERS on the ground that MERS "had no interest in the mortgage being foreclosed and consequently had no standing to bring this action." In Suffolk County, a single judge dismissed four separate MERS cases. In Florida, a Circuit Judge dismissed 20 of them because they had not been "filed by the proper party," and MERS suspended foreclosures in that state. In Connecticut, judges of the Superior Court directed that in any MERS case, no judgment of foreclosure could be entered unless an old-fashioned paper assignment of the mortgage was filed in the land records. We had brought these cases to the attention of the Court of Appeals when we asked it to take the case.

Four years after the Romaine case ended, the New York Times pointed to the "byzantine mortgage securitization process" as a major cause of the "housing bubble" that "allowed home loans to change hands so many times before they were eventually pooled and sold to investors that it is now extremely difficult to track exactly which lenders have claims to a home."

RICHARD C. CAHN

The 2010 University of Cincinnati Law Review article concluded that MERS "did not, by itself, cause the mortgage finance crisis. But it was an important cog in the machine that churned out the millions of unsuitable, poorly underwritten, and incompletely documented mortgages that were destined for foreclosure."

In 2011, the problems with MERS were also highlighted in an article published in the Bankruptcy Reporter, with the intriguing title, The Magic of the Mortgage Electronic Recording System: It Is and It Isn't. Noting that MERS was the "brainchild" of some of the most powerful constituents in the U.S. mortgage investment industry," the article stated that "it quickly became apparent that the MERS model contains a surfeit of problems," among them "the lack of transparency in a historically transparent legal regime." These problems, the author says, "have resulted in mass confusion in the legal arena regarding the proper treatment of MERS." New cases challenging MERS mortgages continued to flood the courts.

Arnold resigned in 2011 as President of MERS. By that year, the press began to focus on MERS. Michael Powell and Gretchen Morgenson of the *New York Times* wrote an article under the captivating caption, "MERS? It May Have Swallowed Your Loan". MERS "could turn out to be a very public problem for the mortgage industry," they stated.

Numbers of judges were now refusing to turn a blind eye to the fact that the MERS foreclosure process did not "comply with the law." The Ohio Secretary of State referred to federal prosecutors accusations that "notaries deputized by MERS were signing hundreds of documents without any personal knowledge of them." A number of courts found that "MERS and its member banks often confused and misrepresented who owned mortgage notes. In thousands of cases, they apparently lost or mistakenly destroyed loan documents."

MAKING LAW

A law professor in Indiana found "fewer than 30 percent of the mortgages had an accurate record in MERS." Even Fannie finally admitted that "we would never rely upon [MERS] to find ownership". MERS began to "advise" its members to record mortgage transfers in county records, after all.

In 2012, the *Times* brought to light a six-year-old investigation of Fannie Mae and MERS that Fannie's Office of Corporate Justice had undertaken in 2006—at the very time we were battling MERS and Fannie in the Court of Appeals. OCJ's 147-page report concluded that attorneys and servicers retained by Fannie and MERS had routinely submitted false foreclosure documents to the courts, evicting people from their homes. The report found that lawyers operating in at least eight states had made false filings on behalf of Fannie Mae or MERS, and that MERS had allowed mortgage proceedings in its name to be brought in states where it was forbidden. By 2011, both Fannie and Freddie had issued regulations forbidding the institution of foreclosure proceedings in MERS's name.

A bankruptcy judge in the Southern District of New York called the failure of the mortgage industry to deal with inaccurate documentation and improper court filings "the greatest failure of lawyering in the last 50 years."

But back in 2006, we lost our case. Without deciding whether the language in the MERS mortgages was legally effective or appropriate, the seven Court of Appeals judges ruled that Romaine, a mere County Clerk, did not have the discretion to reject MERS mortgages or "satisfactions." The Court's decision had consequences, effectively stopping municipal clerks in New York from questioning the validity of any document presented to them, enabling many defective instruments to be recorded, and causing substantial financial losses to many, while countless litigations challenging MERS's practices slowly wended their way through the courts. A sad lesson of the case is, that as comfortable judges might be in exercising "judicial restraint," kicking some cans down the road may not always be beneficial.

However, at least two of the judges were openly troubled. Chief Judge Kaye, contrary to all of her colleagues, wrote that Romaine had specific authority under the law to check the accuracy of mortgage satisfactions before recording them, and that the MERS system made the public record "useless by masking beneficial ownership of mortgages and eliminating records of assignments together". Associate Judge Carmen Ciparek concurred with the majority's ruling, but had misgivings, writing a separate opinion stating that MERS's ambition to hold in its system every mortgage in the nation would "arguably detract from the amount of public data available concerning mortgage ownership that otherwise offers a wealth of statistics that are used to analyze lending practices."

She had obviously noted the important argument in Charney's brief, targeting MERS' documents and procedures as "encouraging predatory lending practices." Judges Kaye and Ciparek both saw a pressing need for the Legislature to amend New York's recording statutes to address the problem. I do not know why the other five judges did not see the same dangers.

Shortly after the decision, bills were introduced in the New York State Legislature to respond to those opinions. If they had become law, they would have authorized county clerks to refuse to record mortgages and related documents that did not preserve the integrity and completeness of the public record. However, the bills were buried, never to see the light of day.

Long after the Romaine case was over and the extent of the mortgage crisis became widely known, I looked again at the Record on Appeal in the Court of Appeals. I took particular notice of the substantial "prepayment" sums that had been paid into MERS in one year by three lenders who had eagerly embraced member-

MAKING LAW

ship in MERS: First Nationwide Mortgage ($412,500); Lehman Brothers ($321,000); and Wells Fargo ($550,000). By then, the first two of these companies had collapsed, and the third lost its independent existence. All were willing participants in the frenzied activities that created the crisis, and all became its victims.

It seems clear now that the MERS mortgage—as its witnesses had testified—had made it possible to create vast and varied bundles of mortgages at lightning speed. And without that ambiguous language in the mortgage, it could never have claimed with a straight face that MERS had the authority to transfer any mortgage to a specified bundle—or anywhere else.

After our appeal was decided in 2006, the courts in a multitude of cases in different states forced MERS to make a number of changes. Borrowers were given access to the MERS system to identify the current owner of their mortgage. MERS continued to designate itself as "mortgagee for recording purposes only," but it no longer had the automatic right to begin foreclosure proceedings; it would in the future be required to take physical possession of the underlying mortgage "note," the "IOU" that a borrower signs to personally assume the debt. Credible proof would need to be submitted to show the Court that the foreclosure plaintiff owned both the note and the mortgage. And the mortgage banking industry said that it would now keeping a closer eye on mortgage brokers and originators to improve the quality of mortgages to be securitized.

In 2018, MERS was acquired by Intercontinental Exchange, the parent company of the New York Stock Exchange. Jeffrey Sprecher, ICE's Chairman and CEO, stated: "As the U.S. mortgage finance industry transitions from a paper-based process to more digital mortgages and electronic notes, MERS is uniquely positioned to provide a seamless process that will bring greater efficiencies to consumers, lenders and institutional investors." I hope that is the case.

RICHARD C. CAHN

The Court of Appeals judges could not have predicted what happened with mortgage securitizations involving MERS mortgages in the 2008 crash, but I think that they had to know, particularly in light of the cases lambasting MERS's practices that were already coming out of the courts in many states, that the wording of the MERS mortgages, and the form of its satisfactions, which certified, without providing proof, that MERS was the current owner of the mortgage, were creating some kind of serious mischief. But in its final decision, the Court ducked the most important legal issue, and that decision had consequences.

Who knows whether the financial crisis would have unfolded in the way it did over the next two years, had New York's prestigious high court ruled in our case that the MERS mortgages did not qualify for recording because they were defective. Such an outcome would have made it difficult, if not impossible, to securitize them in such numbers and at such speeds. That was the clear conclusion to be drawn from MERS's plea to Judge Catterson years before to allow MERS mortgages to be recorded in the form in which they were written, because its "little note and mortgage" was the "lifeblood of the securities industry."

I still wonder if something could have moved the Court to make a contrary decision. I regret that I did not grasp the full implications of the "little note and mortgage" statement. Had I understood and tried to explain the likely consequences, my words would probably have been dismissed as wild speculation. Yet, it is hard not to think, "What if?"

Some years after the Court of Appeals decision and the financial crisis itself, I ran into Judge Kaye at a lawyers' conference and mentioned that I was the lawyer who argued the MERS case before her Court. "Ah, yes, Mr. Cahn, the MERS case," she said, looking directly at me. "I knew there was something wrong with what they were doing but couldn't figure out what it was."

9

DISCRIMINATION AND THE ZONING LAWS: WHAT IS THE "CHARACTER OF THE COMMUNITY" WE ARE PRESERVING?

It is winter 2020, almost 40 years later, and the 14.8-acre property at the northwest corner of Elwood and Pulaski Roads in East Northport still looks as it did in 1980, flat, overgrown with weeds and scrub trees, littered with papers and a few discarded soda cans. Separating the property from the railroad tracks is the Elwood electrical substation with high-voltage power lines, insulators and 10-foot high transformers surrounded by a barbed-wire-topped chain-link fence. Traffic volumes on Pulaski have massively increased, and with every cycle of the Elwood Road stoplight, cars are left behind. The Pulaski Road elementary school occupies the northeast corner of the intersection, and a gasoline station and mini-market are located diagonally across from it on the southwest corner. Beyond the intersection, to the east and south, modest homes are arranged on individual grassy lots, many built in the 1950s but some earlier. A cul-de-sac with somewhat larger homes adjoins the property to the west. On the property, the shrubbery has grown taller, but the neighborhood is still recognizable.

RICHARD C. CAHN

There is no visible indication that this tiny patch of land once generated one of the most bitter court battles Long Island has ever seen, scarring the Huntington, New York, community so deeply that the two sides were still fighting as recently as several months ago.

How easy it is now, to see that in an alternative universe they might have been brought together to actually accomplish something good for the town they all lived in. Instead, a small group of citizens, determined to end what they considered its racial segregation, hired aggressive and experienced counsel, took the town's officials to court, adopted a "take no prisoners" policy that brought out the worst of both sides, and eventually won what looked for four decades like nothing so much as a Pyrrhic victory. On the other side, elected officials with a far different understanding of their duties under New York's zoning laws, strongly defended themselves, and asked the court into which they had been dragged to vindicate the actions that they had taken for years with the legal guidance of the state legislature and the financial support of the federal government. They believed that through the years they had improved the living conditions of countless constituents who were otherwise unable to do that for themselves. In the end, the court system failed, further radicalizing both sides, and the part of the story I was involved in ended with no nationwide legal precedent being created, no solution having been reached, and no closure in sight for anyone on either side.

The town's officials asked me to represent them in that case. I had been involved for years in many zoning litigations where, case by case, the New York courts had been refining the rules that towns and other municipalities would follow as they assigned specific land uses to different parts of their communities. For decades, the courts honored a community's vision for itself, but only if doing so did not unreasonably restrict the use of property so as to deprive its owner of a significant part of its value.

MAKING LAW

From the moment I was retained, I knew that this case would be different: a significant portion of the Huntington community disagreed with its vision, not because someone's property rights were being infringed, but because that vision, embodied in the town's "Comprehensive Plan" and zoning code, effectively prevented them from finding affordable housing outside of the urban renewal area of the town, whose population, by census count, was 52% black.

This shaped up to be one of those historic clashes between titanic forces, and how it ended could well reshape living patterns in all of America. The subject matter was the most sensitive one that the nation had grappled with since its inception: race. It was critical for all the lawyers and judges performing their duties in the case to get it right.

In late August 1980, Marianne Garvin, the Executive Director of a little-known organization called Housing Help, took a last look at a document she had been working on and placed it in an envelope to be mailed to the Department of Housing and Urban Development in Washington. It was an application for federal funding for 162 affordable housing units on the Elwood-Pulaski property, on which Housing Help held an option. The project, if approved, would be called "Matinecock Court."

Garvin was 25 years old, proud possessor of a brand-new Master's degree from the University of Chicago, pregnant with her first child, and almost three years in a job where she truly felt she could make a difference in advancing the cause of racial equality that she passionately believed in.

Garvin came to Long Island to work as an intern with Suffolk Housing Services, a local housing opportunity organization, where she had trained "testers"—pairs of men and women, one pair black, one white—to separately visit the same real estate offices to ask about housing availability for couples in several areas of Suffolk County. She was not surprised to find that racial "steering" was alive and well in the county; many more housing choices were routinely offered to the white "couples" than to the black ones. One of her white "testers" was Robert Ralph, a founder of the organization that was her new employer.

Ralph built houses on Long Island under the name "Quiet Homes," but eventually decided to retire from his business and enjoy his own quiet home in Centerport. He wanted to do something for the community and volunteered to give construction advice to the newly formed Housing Help, which was then applying for government funds to rehabilitate run-down houses in a central area of the town called Huntington Station, that it would deed over to their occupants. The application received the town's blessing, but the federal government turned it down.

The idea for the fledgling organization came from Lloyd Duren, the 43-year old pastor of the Methodist Church on West Neck Road in Huntington. Long dedicated to social action, he had formed a committee of church members to try to find ways to improve housing conditions for the poor and minorities in town, and his activities caught the attention of a small group of Huntington Station residents who were attempting to close down a growing number of illegal apartments in their area. The goals of the two groups meshed, and together they founded Housing Help in 1967.

Another founder was James Lippke, who had previously served the town as a member of its Citizens Housing Advisory Committee, and Chairman of its Housing Authority. Everett Sheldon, the Protestant chaplain at Pilgrim State Hospital, joined the group. He had been active in social causes in the community for more than a decade, speaking to various groups on the role of religion in social relations. In 1968, he joined other local clergymen and representatives of the Huntington Freedom Center and Human Relations Council on a protest march in Washington D.C. in support of the "Poor People's Campaign" that was organized by the Reverend Martin Luther King, Jr. but only took place several weeks after his death.

The organization's Board grew over the ensuing years. Ralph joined, as did several other community residents: Lawrence McNally, a psychologist in the Northport school system; Elizabeth Norton, the director of a pre-school operating out of the Congregational Church in Centerport; and Fredericka Gilroy, a member of that church. On workdays, wearing her hat as a real estate agent, Gilroy tried to help people in the town's minority population find homes. Bernard "Bud" Peyton, a highly-regarded engineer and executive with a local aircraft instrumentation manufacturer, was active in the Methodist Church and joined Duren's committee. Maurice Perkins became the first black member.

Ralph, in a telephone conversation in 2013, told me about his former colleagues in the early days of Housing Help and about the evolution of their thinking over the years. He agreed to meet me soon in person to continue our discussion. However, a few days later he told me that he had changed his mind about cooperating in the writing of this chapter; he no longer thought it was "appropriate" for him to share information with me, since the construction of low income housing at the Elwood-Pulaski site was still in litigation—it was then 25 years after it had initially been approved by the courts. At one point in our telephone discussion, he told me that he thought Housing Help might finally put a shovel in the ground before the end of that year, and he hoped that whenever it was, he'd be "vertical" and on hand to see it. But it was not to be: in January 2017, four years after our talk, he died at the age of 93.

Marianne Garvin and former town officials also shared with me their recollections of the years before and after Garvin sent off the HUD funding application in the summer of 1980.

Huntington Station, the first focus of Housing Help's efforts, had a long history, shaped by its longtime connection to the Long

Island Rail Road. In 1868, the LIRR tracks finally extended the entire 36 miles from Pennsylvania Station and reached Huntington, and jobs near any terminal on the line would now be accessible to those without private transportation. As a result, housing for immigrants and the poor became concentrated in the area within walking distance of the station. Elsewhere in the town were scattered small farms and privately-owned single-family homes.

Time took its toll on the Huntington Station housing: by the 1960s, buildings on both sides of the tracks had badly deteriorated. The town applied for federal funds under the new Urban Renewal program, and again later under the Community Development Block Grant program, and was awarded millions of dollars to rehabilitate the area. In 13 years, the town created 330 new units of subsidized housing, all in Huntington Station, and approved by the government.

The town's officials thought that they had done a good job of creating apartments in an area where they were clearly needed. Organizations assisting poor and minority citizens, including Housing Help and the NAACP, were also happy with the town's efforts. In 1976, the Central Long Island Branch of the NAACP told the government that it was "very pleased with the way Huntington has proposed to use its grant as a catalyst for housing and community rehabilitation." Housing Help praised the fact that five "target" areas chosen for residential rehabilitation in Huntington Station were "all blighted neighborhoods with a high concentration of minority and low-income persons." In 1978, Housing Help told HUD the town's Community Development Block Grant application was "exemplary for its emphasis on rehabilitation and appears clearly designed to assist low and moderate income persons."

When two years later, Garvin mailed out the HUD funding application for the Elwood/Pulaski property, Housing Help would no longer praise the "exemplary" nature of the town's Huntington Station projects. It now focused its attention on the fact that the apartment construction allowed by the town was in an area that was 52 percent minority, mostly black, while the areas outside of Huntington Station were overwhelmingly white. In its public statements, it now labeled Huntington Station a "racial ghetto," and claimed that the town's zoning plan had intentionally excluded blacks and other minorities from those outlying areas. Housing Help would now try to open up those areas to all.

When Huntington's Town Board members learned of the HUD application, they did not understand Housing Help's dramatic change from strongly supporting the town's development efforts in Huntington Station to opposing them. That shift, which was never explained by Housing Help, substantially contributed to the later hostility between it and the town. In retrospect, it seems clear that Housing Help was one of many affordable housing organizations that faced a dilemma: whether to pour their resources into the improvement of residential areas that were in fact segregated, or instead push for changes that would result in greater integration. At some point, their priorities changed.

In conversations with me years later, Garvin's own description of that period was dramatic: there were "powerful forces keeping people in their place," she said.

During Housing Help's start-up years, Lippke became particularly active and by 1980 he, too, had dramatically changed his views of the town's officials who had once been his patrons. When, years earlier, he had accepted the town's appointment to the housing advisory committee, he believed that the local zoning laws favoring apartments in the Huntington Station area had been adopted for good public policy reasons. He had joined his colleagues on the advisory committee who publicly stated that they saw "no conflict" between encouraging development of affordable

RICHARD C. CAHN

housing and preserving "the desirable and cherished characteristics of our community."

By 1980, however, Lippke was disgusted, writing to the editor of the Long Islander, the local weekly newspaper, that "the major obstacle" to an increase in housing for the poor "at all times has been elected officials who privately admit to the need but who won't put their job on the line for fear of losing the next election." His disillusionment with the town's policies strongly influenced the other members of Housing Help's organization.

In the fall of 1979, Housing Help asked Alan Mallach, a planning consultant who was already working with Suffolk Housing Services, to identify a "desirable" site for affordable housing. He was to use only a single criterion: the property had to be in an area with "an almost entirely white population." He followed the instruction carefully: the area surrounding the corner of Elwood and Pulaski Roads was 98% white.

No in-depth traffic study or identification and analysis of other positive and negative features of the site was ever performed. Many studies would have been required for an actual rezoning application. Housing Help's board thought none were necessary because the organization had no intention of filing such an application. In fact, its leaders later testified that they did not know that a zoning application would be required.

Learning that the property was owned by Max Staller, a well-known Long Island real estate developer and generous contributor to charitable causes, Garvin contacted Staller's grandson, who was managing his affairs. By late January, with the help of Morton Willen, a volunteer local attorney, the group negotiated an option to buy the property. The only request made by the Staller family was that Housing Help should pay the real estate taxes on the property until it decided whether it would exercise its option to buy it. The application that Garvin placed in the mail the following August advised HUD that the new complex would be "25 percent minority."

The application was certain to attract public attention: the project could not be built unless the Town Board agreed to change the property's zoning classification, and that could not be done under State law without conducting a public hearing.

Huntington had great natural attractions. There were five beautiful harbors, and the Connecticut shoreline was clearly visible a dozen miles across Long Island Sound. There was a great deal of open space, and since enacting the town's first zoning ordinance in the 1930s, its officials had taken pains to preserve as much of it as they could by means of careful zoning and planning restrictions. As was (and still is) typical, zoning laws separated commercial and industrial activities from residential areas, residential districts could be classified as single-family or multi-family, and different lot area requirements applied in differently zoned "districts." Since the 1960s, the town had encouraged apartment construction in Huntington Station, but had not provided for apartment construction in other areas of the town, unless by the town's own Housing Authority.

People liked community development to be guided by the principles of planning and zoning, so they could live in a house in an area designated for similar homes, rather than in a community that had developed in helter-skelter fashion, where they might find themselves living next to an industrial power plant, a busy business district, or a utility plant with an active smokestack. The laws that embodied such zoning and planning concepts were validated by the Supreme Court in 1925 in an Ohio case called Euclid v. Ambler. A town's preferences for the way its communities should be laid out, were thereafter given great deference by the courts. That kind of planning had produced suburban communities like Huntington.

RICHARD C. CAHN

The town was founded in the early 1600s, and even today, there are residents who trace their ancestors back to the American Revolution. In the years following World War II, the town became a prime destination for young families, mostly white, seeking to move from New York City's five boroughs to Long Island's open space. Huntington's population exploded, growing from 47,506 in 1950 to 197,089 in 1980, of whom 187,794 were whites, 6,183 were blacks, 4,666 Hispanics, and 2,445 Asians. The black population represented 3.35% of the total.

The residents—even the new arrivals who had contributed to it—were concerned about the consequences of rapid growth. They attended public hearings to monitor the actions of the town's elected officials and they did not hesitate to invoke New York State general laws and the town's own planning policies and zoning provisions—which many had taken the time to study—to plead for "the preservation of our quality of life." State laws explicitly directed towns, villages and cities considering planning and zoning actions and various other actions requiring environmental study, not to make them without specifically taking into account preservation of "the character of the community."

By the mid-19th century, the town's population included a small number of black families, who in 1843 founded the Bethel AME Church on Park Avenue in Huntington Village, where services were regularly conducted for the next 163 years. Some members came to Huntington in the first part of the 19th century to labor in Crossman Brickyards, near Long Island Sound in what became known as Lloyd Harbor; before the church was founded, prayer meetings and religious services were held in the homes of members living in the Wall Street area of Huntington village. By 1980, the black population of the town mostly lived in Huntington Station and a small area of Greenlawn, about two miles to the east. In 2006, the Bethel AME congregation moved to New York Avenue in Huntington Station.

MAKING LAW

The view—literally, the perspective—of black residents in Huntington Station toward the town's zoning laws at that time was far less supportive than that of the town's white residents. The Station, even with all the urban renewal and community development changes, was still a heavily commercialized area cut in two by a busy railroad line and terminal, with three nearby apartment "projects" that had been constructed with federal money, many of whose inhabitants were receiving financial assistance under such initiatives as the Section 8 program.

A large percentage of the inhabitants in the three subsidized housing projects in the Station were minority. In 1984, in Gateway Gardens, 38 of 40 units were occupied by blacks or Hispanics; in Whitman Village, 56% of the families were minority; and in Lincoln Manor, 30% of the households and 45% of those on the waiting list were minority. Sixty-eight percent of those holding Section 8 certificates in the town and 61% on its waiting list, were minority.

The individual plaintiffs in the case were three African-American residents of Huntington Station, who were in difficult circumstances. Two told their stories from the witness stand. Perrepper Crutchfield had been employed for more than 20 years as a medical technician at SUNY Stony Brook and later at Northport VA Hospital, making $17,500 per year when she left the latter position. She had been living for more than 20 years either in subsidized housing or in her parents' home. At the time of trial she lived in a two-room ground floor apartment in Lincoln Manor in Huntington Station with two daughters, one of whom was 25 years of age. Ms. Crutchfield was paying $351 in rent. Kenneth Cofield had a wife and four children, and the family lived at various locations through the years, at times together and at times with relatives at separate locations. He lost his job with the Town's highway department. A Section 8 certificate entitled him to a subsidy of $468 per month, and at the time of trial he was paying rent of $229.

The post-war residents of the town had been dissatisfied with their former living conditions in or near New York City, and were able to move to Huntington. In 1980, the individual plaintiffs were unhappy with their living conditions in Huntington Station, but there did not seem to be any practical way that they could move to another part of the town at all.

On the basis of census figures showing minority racial concentration in Huntington Station, Housing Help charged the town with violating the Fair Housing Act by "perpetuating" racial segregation.

The town's defense case was harder to personalize, as the question for the court was more academic: was it accurate or fair to characterize the town's efforts to rehabilitate Huntington Station by encouraging builders to construct new apartments, as "perpetuating segregation," and did the Fair Housing Act impose upon the town an affirmative obligation to locate apartment buildings in other areas that had long been set aside for single-family residences, thereby changing their "character?"

The local newspapers chronicled the hostility of the residents to apartment construction. An article covering a Northport Village Board meeting reported how a typical public hearing on apartment construction in those days would go: "A large and vociferous segment" of village residents crowded into the meeting to demand that "apartment construction should be banned" pending adoption of a master zoning plan. One resident complained that "the master plan will take two years to complete. We could have a lot of apartment houses built here in two years, and we wouldn't be able to get them out."

Huntington's elected officials—many of whom had themselves relocated from the City—were well aware that there was significant opposition in the community toward apartment construction, and shared it. However, there was a strong demand for rental housing, and illegal apartments popped up all over town in scattered basements, spare bedrooms and unused garages. The only legal "multi-family dwellings" before 1967 were several aged brick structures which served as apartment buildings, laid out along two streets on the outskirts of the business district in Huntington village. They were "grandfathered" in, because they pre-existed zoning restrictions in that area.

In 1980, Huntington's Town Code and Zoning Map showed two zoning classifications in the areas near the Elwood-Pulaski property on which Housing Help wished to build. One area was "R-40", requiring a one-acre plot for each house, and another was "R-5", meaning that a single-family house could be built on a 5,000 square foot lot.

Towns sometimes designated blighted parts of the municipality as urban renewal areas, where residents urgently needed housing assistance, and those special use areas had been seen by federal housing officials and local government officials as beneficial to the residents. Huntington's town government created an urban renewal area in Huntington Station, and thereafter continued to develop that area under the new Community Development Block Grant program. HUD, the federal Department of Housing and Urban Development, prescribed the rules for development and funded it.

Urban Renewal and Community Development programs eventually fell into disfavor. Andrew Wiese, in his book *Places of Their Own*, specifically wrote about Bennington Park, a mostly black enclave in Freeport, the village where I grew up. Wiese said Freeport "knocked down 250 dwellings and replaced them with only 100 units of low income housing on an out-of-the-way site a short distance away." Some, sarcastically but accurately, referred to Urban Renewal as "Negro Renewal."

Unlike Freeport, Huntington took the government's money and by all accounts used it properly. Starting in the 1950s the town used federal funds to rehabilitate and replace a number of buildings in Huntington Station. McNally, then Housing Help's president, pointed out in a 1981 newsletter that the town had at that point accepted "more than $7,000,000 of community development funds in the last five years." The town received funding to construct apartments for low-income families, and amended its zoning code to encourage apartment construction in the Station.

But the latter provision became a problem for Housing Help, not because of what it said, but because of what it did not say. The organization claimed that the town excluded apartments anywhere except in the Station. Although that was technically incorrect (one of the town's agencies, the Housing Authority, was free under the zoning code to build low-income rental units anywhere in town, but private developers had to seek a zoning change to do so), it was accurate in describing the way development had actually played out.

By 1980, Housing Help changed its focus, and would no longer support rehabilitation efforts in Huntington Station. Instead, it would try to force the town to allow apartments in predominantly white areas. That new goal would inevitably clash with the Town Board's concentration on rehabilitating and building apartments inside the Station, and that conflict would be greatly exacerbated by another event.

The town's shortage of affordable housing for senior citizens had become evident in 1960, with the issuance of a report by the town's Citizens Housing Committee, authored in part by future Housing Help board member Lippke. The town's Planning Department had also reported that 60% of families in Huntington with a head of household 65 years of age had an annual income of less than $5,000.

In 1965, the Conference of the Methodist Church, of which Reverend Duren's church in Huntington was, ironically, a member, had asked the town to create a new "Retirement Community District," for property the church group owned in East Northport. In response, the Town Board created a "Retirement" zoning district, "R-RM." Housing Help publicly commended the town for creating the "retirement" zone.

The town was then receiving ten inquiries per day from elderly persons in need of housing and had a file of more than 400 requests from seniors to be placed on the waiting list for the 292 units that the Methodist Conference wished to build. The town's Director of Senior Citizen Programs said that more than 2,000 senior citizens were unable to find adequate housing in Huntington within their means.

Nearby residents were opposed to apartments of any kind and sued to undo what the town had done. After *nine years* of litigation, the State Court of Appeals upheld the town's action, concluding "that there was considerable and justifiable community concern" over the lack of housing for the aged. The Town Board, finally free to do so, rezoned the Church's parcel on Pulaski Road (less than a mile from the Housing Help property) for "Paumanok Village," the first senior citizen apartment complex in the town. The neighbors went back to court to challenge the rezoning of the Church property, and lost again.

So, finally, in 1975, fifteen years after the town's Senior Citizens Housing Committee had rendered its report, Paumanok Village was underway.

Five years after the end of the senior citizens litigation, Housing Help prepared to bring its lawsuit against the town. Its first step was to confront town Board members with a proposal that those officials knew nothing about and did not see coming.

RICHARD C. CAHN

In March 1980, Garvin called the Town Board office and proposed a "get together" meeting between its members and representatives of Housing Help. Instead of being a social meeting, it led to the filing 11 months later of a major federal civil rights case against the town by Housing Help and the Huntington Branch of the NAACP.

Four members of the Town Board met with Ralph, Garvin and Lippke. The presence of Lippke, well known to the town's officials from his appointment years before to the housing advisory committee, initially reassured them that the meeting would not present any hidden dangers, but they were wrong.

Giving no advance hint of their purpose, Housing Help's representatives began the meeting by announcing that they had obtained an option on property located at the corner of Elwood and Pulaski Roads, which they believed was appropriate for low income apartments, and they now wanted the Board to rezone it for multi-family housing. And, they said, the location was "non-negotiable."

The four Town Board members felt "sandbagged," and red flags went up for another reason: New York's "Open Meetings Law" prohibited a quorum of the Board (three members out of five) from discussing or transacting town business except in a public meeting.

Even if there had been no Open Meetings Law, the Board members were not in a position to give Housing Help the assurances it sought, because State law required a formal rezoning application, accompanied by detailed surveys, maps and extensive environmental studies, to be submitted to the town before any rezoning request could be considered.

The town's officials tried to make one point clear: if Housing Help wanted a rezoning of any property, they "had to follow proper zoning procedures," but that advice fell on uncomprehending ears. At the trial years later, Housing Help's leaders admitted they had not known what "zoning procedures" were.

MAKING LAW

This was very hard to believe when it came out that two days before the "get together" meeting, Garvin, Janet Hanson of Suffolk Housing Services, and Alan Mallach, a zoning consultant, had met with Richard Bellman, a well-known civil rights lawyer from Manhattan, to discuss the lawsuit that Housing Help intended to file against the town if it did not accede to its demands. The Housing Help people had been in a room with a zoning expert who could have explained in detail what would be required of them, but nobody asked.

Garvin told me years later that she had become uncomfortable with Housing Help's confrontational approach even before she filed the HUD application; apparently she had been particularly disturbed by that meeting with the Town Board members.

Garvin also disagreed with her Board's refusal a year later to support additional multi-family housing in Huntington Station, even when the town proposed resolving the dispute by allowing the construction of an equal number of new units inside and outside of the Station area. The disagreement led to Garvin's resignation from the organization.

Thirty-three years later when we talked, Garvin had been serving for more than a third of that time as President and CEO of the Community Development Corporation, an extraordinarily successful not-for-profit organization seeking to expand affordable housing everywhere on Long Island. By then, she firmly believed that the tactic of attempting to "strong-arm" elected officials was both ineffective and wrong.

In twelve years under Garvin's presidency, CDC had built more than 1,000 units of affordable and elderly housing in Nassau and Suffolk counties, and she deserved considerable credit for the accomplishment; she and her CDC colleagues had been following a different scenario: they identified towns needing affordable housing, discussed those needs with community leaders, and kept

RICHARD C. CAHN

an open mind about alternative housing locations. They considered it important to use persuasion rather than coercion, and had remarkable success.

CDC's results sharply contrasted with Housing Help's in the Huntington case, which after seven years of litigation resulted in a federal court directive to rezone the Elwood-Pulaski property, but failure for decades afterwards to build a single unit of affordable housing at the site.

In our later conversations, Garvin framed the choice facing such organizations as, "do you want to sue, or do you want to build housing?"

The initial hostile encounter between Housing Help and the Town Board members had essentially destroyed the possibility of a constructive or cooperative approach to affordable housing. Thereafter, whatever one side did was viewed as underhanded by the other.

Several days after that meeting, the Town Board held a public hearing on the town's proposed 1980-81 application for Community Development funds. Ralph addressed the entire Board, saying that his organization had "a number of suggestions" for the application, but rather than summarize the organization's "ideas," he handed the Town Clerk a single copy of a voluminous document, which was filed after the meeting in the town's offices. Long afterward it was discovered that buried deep inside the document was a "recommendation" that the town amend the zoning code to allow apartments outside of the Huntington Station area. The group later argued that the document was a rezoning application.

Butterfield, the town's Supervisor and chief executive, only learned about the February "get-together" meeting six months afterwards, when he received a copy of Garvin's letter informing HUD that Housing Help would be submitting a request for funds for Matinecock Court. He immediately consulted with James

MAKING LAW

Dunne, the town's Director of Community Development and Harold Letson, its long-time Planning Director.

Dunne was the official who advised the Town Board on the Community Development program and was a key participant in the annual meetings between the town and HUD in which the town's Housing Assistance Plan, containing its housing goals for the ensuing year, was discussed and hopefully agreed to. Letson was the town's chief professional planner; he oversaw the review of all development proposals in the town to ensure that they conformed to the town's zoning laws and its "Comprehensive Plan" that was required by State law.

Both men advised Butterfield that the proposed site was unsuitable for the project. Located far outside the areas served by the sewer district and the town's transportation system, they predicted serious traffic and sewage disposal issues. It was also inconsistent with the town's latest HAP.

The town's Housing Authority, the operator of low-income housing in the Station, also questioned the viability of the proposal. Butterfield prepared a letter summarizing the town's concerns and considered it so important that he personally delivered it in mid-October to HUD offices in Manhattan.

It was at that point that Housing Help's plan became public, and East Northport reacted in a fury. A protest meeting of a new neighborhood organization, calling itself "Concerned Citizens," was hastily put together by an East Northport resident, Joan Flowers, and drew more than 1,000 residents. A hand-lettered poster reminiscent of 18th Century pre-Revolution "broadsides," was introduced with capital letters: "RESIDENTS URGENT!!—HUD LOW INCOME HOUSING PROPOSAL RESIDENTS OF EAST NORTHPORT, NORTHPORT AND GREENLAWN." It was placed in mailboxes throughout the area, announcing a meeting to be held at the Old Fields Jr. High School on November 6. The headline in the following week's issue of The Long Islander read "Spillover Crowd Opposes Subsidized Housing Plan."

Flowers was an unlikely leader of an organization formed to thwart an affordable housing project intended mainly to serve minorities, as she herself was black.

Passions of the East Northport community were inflamed. The Town Hall switchboard lit up, and pressures on the Town Board members to state their position on the housing proposal ratcheted up. Mutterings were heard that any town official voting for the plan would be turned out of office. Butterfield let it be known that he had written to HUD to oppose the project but failed to cool the community's anger.

Any hope that the discussion was going to develop in a calm, measured way virtually disappeared at the moment the community learned about the project. That hope might have been rekindled, had the Town Board members remained silent about the proposal until they had before them a formal rezoning application that they could carefully study, but they didn't.

As the crowd gathered for the Concerned Citizens meeting, a petition opposing the Housing Help project began to circulate, and eventually collected 4,100 signatures.

Butterfield had initially decided not to attend the meeting. He was worried about being provoked into saying something he would later regret, and he told his fellow Town Board members they would also be better advised to stay away. But as public pressure built, Butterfield failed to follow his own advice. On November 6, he drove over to the school building. Every Board member except Councilman Kenneth Deegan attended the meeting. State Assemblyman John Flanagan and State Senator James Lack also attended, although neither of them had any official role in local zoning decisions.

The crowd demanded to know what position each official would take. One by one, they took the microphone and stated their opposition. Butterfield read his letter to HUD aloud. Councilman Deegan later told a Long Islander reporter that "the town opposed the project," but would facilitate it if Housing Help would build it in Huntington Station.

The Town Board was scheduled to have a regular public meeting on January 6, 1981, and Councilman Deegan, a conservative Republican lawyer who spoke bluntly and played "hard ball" politics, had a surprise for Butterfield. He had prepared a resolution plainly stating that the Board opposed the proposal and shared it with his Republican colleagues on the Board, but not with Butterfield.

Thus, Butterfield knew nothing about Deegan's resolution until just before walking into the Board meeting room, and he had no opportunity to discuss it privately; now, he felt "sandbagged," but there was nothing he could do about it.

The Town Board was bitterly split, with three Republicans and two Democrats; the two factions had been warring against each other for months. The prior autumn, the GOP majority seized financial control of the town's budget from Butterfield, ignoring Butterfield's role as the town's Chief Financial Officer.

Rumors of imminent layoffs of town employees had been circulating, each faction blaming the other. By October 23, the town had to borrow to pay its operating expenses, and in late November angry employees were carrying protest signs at Town Board meetings; within a month, 65 town employees were laid off.

How much hostility with Butterfield played into the decision to keep him in the dark about the Deegan resolution, is unknown, but the maneuver cut off any opportunity for the members to discuss the matter privately or consult with the Town Attorney before adopting the resolution, decisions that prejudiced the town in the federal case—probably fatally.

RICHARD C. CAHN

On January 6, the Town Hall auditorium in the old Huntington High School building on Main Street was packed with residents; every seat was occupied; people crowded into the auditorium behind the circular array of seats and spilled into the hallway. Butterfield, seething after seeing the Deegan resolution, tried to make a statement in measured, lawyer-like fashion, hoping to calm the crowd. Later he remembered his remarks as a fairly effective explanation of the lengthy process Housing Help would have to go through to obtain a zoning change, and thought he had reassured the audience that each of them would have ample opportunity to express their concerns before any decision would be made. The Second Circuit judges would later label him the "principal speaker" in opposition to the project. Deegan's resolution was adopted, and Butterfield, "sandbagged" or not, joined the others in voting to approve it.

By adopting that resolution, the Town Board placed on record its rejection of affordable housing at Housing Help's site. I cringed when I found the official "Resolution" in the town's files, which the Town Clerk had duly stamped as having been unanimously adopted. The Board members had even spelled out the specific zoning-related reasons why they considered the site inappropriate.

The resolution had trouble written all over it, and if they did not already know about it, Housing Help's lawyers would sooner or later have a copy.

For the sake of political posturing and in one hasty action, the Town Board rejected a Housing Help application that had never been made, thus making it possible for Housing Help to argue, successfully, that there was no need to file one, because the Board had decided to reject it without seeing it.

When Housing Help learned of Deegan's resolution, its members must have raised a glass to thank the town officials for falling into a trap of their own making. Three weeks later, Housing

MAKING LAW

Help, joined by the Huntington Branch of the NAACP, a co-plaintiff with nationwide name recognition, filed their long-planned lawsuit, based in part upon the town's "refusal" to rezone the East Northport property.

Housing Help's directors had solidified their views that the town's entire zoning plan was discriminatory, and that racial prejudice was at the root of the town's hostility to low-income housing. The January 6 resolution confirmed their worst suspicions.

I was generally supportive of land development decisions that Huntington had made through the years to safeguard the town's beauty and charm. Huntington's officials had done a great deal to preserve open air and green space. But Housing Help's new lawsuit was raising issues that affected many more communities than Huntington, which, in its layout, and its attitudes toward apartments, was similar to a great many other towns. The courts, from the Supreme Court on down, had sanctified planning and zoning practices that Huntington and those other communities had followed for many years. Housing Help's lawsuit was aimed squarely at residential segregation in America; it was effectively asking the courts to declare all American suburbs illegal.

When I was retained by the town, I was struck by the enormous scope of my assignment. I knew that Huntington Station had become a preferred location for apartments because they were needed there, but the judges who would hear the case would not know of that history unless we told them about it. I hoped I would be able to prove that the town's planning and zoning decisions through the years were not based upon race; in the lawsuit the Town was accused of intentionally discriminating against blacks and other minorities; I did not think that was true, but I needed to be sure.

I began the slow work of analyzing hundreds of files relating to land development decisions that the town had made through the years. The case forced me not only to look more critically at the town's earlier zoning decisions, but also to reevaluate in light of the Fair Housing Act, the federal law under which Housing Help sued the town, all of the principles of zoning law that I thought I knew well.

I was concerned about the history of Paumanok Village. That senior citizens complex was on Pulaski Road a short distance east of the Housing Help property, and against great community opposition the Town Board had facilitated that project in every way possible, which, it could be argued, sharply contrasted with its negative reaction to Housing Help's. Yet it cut the other way that for nine years the East Northport neighbors had fought against Paumanok, a development that was never expected to have a significant minority population, which tended to show that the community's opposition to apartments was motivated by factors other than racial bias.

It was also in the town's favor that the thousands of pages of government forms and supporting documents that had led to the construction and government financing for low-income apartments in Huntington Station, and for Paumanok, showed that all of those projects, unlike Housing Help's, were consistent with federal guidelines, and were being processed after formal applications, with close attention to the town's zoning and environmental requirements.

I thought it was a strange development that the Town Board was being accused of acting on the basis of racial bias to build more low-income housing in a part of town where it had been located for close to 100 years. If Housing Help's lawyers were right, the Fair Housing Act had changed everything I had ever learned about zoning.

I went to talk to Butterfield. His political enemies said he "looked like a Boy Scout." I agreed that he did, but thought he

MAKING LAW

ought to take it as a compliment. He was a fellow lawyer from my early Huntington village days, and I thought he was what he looked like: a youthful idealist with a scrubbed face and a warm smile, the antithesis of the archetypical back room politician. He and I both loved jazz, and on several occasions, I was listening when he played his trumpet somewhere in town with a small Dixieland band he had organized. As I drove to Town Hall to talk with him, there was no way I thought that he was a bigot. I felt that his likeability and sincerity would impress the trial judge.

Butterfield was troubled about the inflammatory Concerned Citizens petition and the letters and telephone calls protesting the Housing Help proposal that were flooding Town Hall. He understood clearly that he was required to make official decisions fairly and on the merits, but as Huntington's highest elected official, he had to listen carefully to his constituents on a variety of pending actions and take their views into account.

Those two imperatives of public office could work against each other but Butterfield thought that he could manage the conflict and make his decisions dispassionately.

I did not know if, or to what degree, the residents involved in the Concerned Citizens group opposing the Matinecock Court were motivated by racial prejudice. I thought it was difficult to say that about Flowers, the organization's founder, because of her own race. However, the trial judge in our case would be duty-bound to carefully explore the motivations of all the actors. He would take a close look at how the "Concerned Citizens" had acted, and would have to decide whether they were significantly motivated by racial hostility. If he found that the Town Board members' official actions were in any way tainted by bias, their own or others', we would lose the case. This would be a non-jury trial, and the trial judge's evaluation would be critical. Any finding regarding the presence or absence of bias would be based upon the judge's personal observation and evaluation of the witnesses who testified before him in his courtroom. If normal judicial practice prevailed, appeals judges—who would not see the witnesses at all—would not second-guess him.

I needed to personally interview all the official town actors and try to judge their motivations for myself. A lot of the hostility that I heard about Housing Help was traceable to the so-called "get together" meeting, which I spent a lot of time discussing with those who were there.

There was another, curious angle to the case. New York State was not involved in the lawsuit, but its statewide zoning policies were very much implicated in the dispute. The State required that a local government considering a zoning action determine whether it would "preserve the character" of a neighborhood. If the Court in our case required the town to open existing single-family neighborhoods to apartment zoning, it would necessarily be declaring the State's policy, as well as Huntington's, a violation of the Fair Housing Act.

To their credit, Housing Help and their lawyer Bellman did not in the end try to prove intentional discrimination on the part of the town; their witnesses testified that they believed the comments of the Town Board members at the "get acquainted" meeting were "political," but not "discriminatory." I. Leo Glasser, the trial judge, ruled that there was no evidence that the actions of the town's officials were racially motivated, and his finding was never disturbed on appeal.

But that was only the beginning of the fight. The Fair Housing Act could be interpreted to outlaw actions that had a discriminatory "effect" or "impact." Congress had never specified whether the law was intended only to address housing decisions motivated by racial hostility, or whether, as two federal circuit courts had already ruled, actions having a discriminatory "effect" or "impact" violated the law; and the federal law prohibiting discrimination in employment had already been interpreted to cover actions that had discriminatory impact.

Glasser, well-respected at the bench and bar, was a scholarly former Brooklyn Law School dean and professor who was very new to the bench. Although he had only become a judge 10 months after the case was filed, it seemed that his instincts and temperament would strongly incline him toward careful study and deliberation. In my view, he was a perfect judge for the case.

Richard Bellman, my adversary, a former staff lawyer for the U.S. Civil Rights Commission, was well known as a zealous and effective advocate for civil rights. He was the partner of another civil rights lawyer, Lewis Steel, in their small Manhattan law firm. Steel and Bellman had successfully pursued a number of civil rights actions in the metropolitan area, including extensive litigation against Mt. Laurel, New Jersey that set aside land regulations which had obstructed the establishment of affordable housing for the poor. I was taken aback when Bellman made clear in our first meeting that he considered me to be his "enemy," rather than his adversary. I did not know whether his attitude represented his actual feelings or were merely a psychological tactic. Whatever his mindset, I knew he was highly-skilled and had extensive experience in the civil rights field.

The discriminatory effect argument had been raised in Bellman's Mt. Laurel cases, and we expected part of this case to be based upon a similar claim. I had to be fully prepared to rebut any claim that Huntington's zoning provisions had a discriminatory "effect."

But it could be personally unpleasant at times to litigate against Bellman. At one point I was taking a deposition of an NAACP official at Bellman's office, and excluded Stewart Moore from the room. Moore was a young black intern employed by the NAACP at the time, and I was considering calling him as a potential witness to contradict the testimony of the official I was questioning. Bellman had no legal grounds to refuse my request to exclude him but took the occasion to call me a "racist" for having done so. Several years after that, as we both entered the ornate courtroom of the U. S. Court of Appeals for the Second Circuit in Foley Square in Manhattan to argue his appeal from Judge Glasser's dismissal of his case, Bellman leaned toward me, and muttered to my face, "I'm going to crush you!"

Years later, in talking to Ralph and Garvin, I learned that it was Bellman who had shot down a possible compromise with the town that would have involved construction of additional low-income housing, in and outside of Huntington Station, but not on the Elwood-Pulaski site. This was in every meaning of the phrase, a "test case."

Garvin's take, years later, was that "the case had become everything."

The Fair Housing Act prohibits the denial of housing to any individual because of race. In the end, the Second Circuit judges determined that both of the claims against Huntington—that the town violated the law by excluding apartments from any area other than Huntington Station, and by rejecting Housing Help's specific request for rezoning of the Elwood-Pulaski property (which it had never made)—would be governed by the "effects" or "impact" test, because, they said, "every disparate impact case would include a disparate treatment component." My research had persuaded me otherwise, but that part of the Court's decision was well within the customary limits of judicial interpretation of a law.

Making a record that the town's actions did not have a discriminatory "impact" or "effect" proved to be elusive, as the favored method of showing that was to perform a statistical analysis, and the Huntington statistics could be used to prove either proposition. In fact, Judge Glasser and later the Circuit Court of Appeals used those same numbers and came to opposite conclu-

MAKING LAW

sions. Glasser ruled that the evidence of discriminatory effect was "not particularly strong" because the *number* of whites (22,160) far exceeded the *number* of blacks, Hispanics and Asians (3,671) who would be eligible to live in the proposed project, and therefore the impact of a denial by the town would fall disproportionately upon the white population. However, the Second Circuit judges compared the *percentages* of each race that would be disadvantaged by a deprivation of housing, and found a disproportionate impact upon blacks and other minorities.

We highlighted Housing Help's amateur efforts to obtain their desired zoning changes. When the time came for her to testify, Marianne Garvin was recovering from the delivery of her son, and she appeared in Brooklyn only by videotape, her earnest face appearing on a large screen in the courtroom. She did not equivocate; what she said established that Housing Help had not at any time familiarized itself with the town's Comprehensive Plan or discussed the housing proposal with town's planners.

Ralph, by then Housing Help's Chairman, took the witness stand, and testified that "it never occurred to me that there was any problem" with meeting privately with Town Board members and attempting to transact official business away from public scrutiny—activity that New York's Open Meetings Law prohibited. He didn't "believe that he knew" in 1980 that a formal zoning application was required. Glasser was persuaded, and after the trial ended, he wrote a long opinion dismissing the case, and our adversaries immediately filed an appeal.

And Bellman's prediction turned out to be correct; he crushed us.

I was disappointed but not surprised that the three Circuit Court judges settled on the "effects" or "impact" test, in part because proving discriminatory intent is a very difficult proposition: people rarely admit their prejudices, and "smoking guns" are rare.

Using numbers showing that those receiving Section 8 assistance and on its waiting list were 60% minority, the appeals judges

RICHARD C. CAHN

concluded that minorities were disproportionately affected by Huntington's failure to permit apartments outside of Huntington Station. The case established legal precedent, but only for the Second Circuit.

I disagreed with, and was disappointed by, the Circuit judges' decision, but it had always been a possible outcome.

It was a stunning surprise, however, to see the appeal judges strip Glasser of a trial judge's traditional power to devise a remedy for the wrong committed. They chose to directly impose one themselves, ordering the Town Board to rezone the Elwood-Pulaski property to permit apartment construction. They gave Housing Help "site-specific" relief, which, considering that no specific application had ever been filed, was in reality a blank check, but for many years, it turned out to be worthless.

Had the Circuit judges left it to Judge Glasser to perform his customary duty to devise a remedy, he could have afforded the parties the opportunity to discuss the suitability of a number of alternative sites outside of the racially concentrated area of Huntington Station, which after the Second Circuit decision were no longer off-limits for apartments. The stage would have been set for a serious discussion, and a real possibility of a settlement of the case that would have enabled the immediate construction of the needed housing. The "test case" would have produced a helpful result for real people.

But the appeal judges had ruled with such a heavy hand that they foreclosed discussion of the merits of alternative sites. They conceded that "ordinarily" they would have sent the matter back to the trial judge to afford the town "an opportunity to identify an alternative site." They gave three reasons for their not doing so: that the case had been going on for seven years and "further delay might well prove fatal to this developer's plans"; that the town "has demonstrated little good faith in assisting the development of low-income housing;" and that no land outside of Huntington Station was then zoned for multi-family housing.

Our view was that both sides were equally responsible for the delay in the case, and it was unfair to punish the town by implicitly blaming it for that delay; the evidence of HUD's "pressuring" the town to include commitments for subsidized family housing (the Court's basis for questioning the town's good faith), was merely an example of the annual haggling between any municipality and HUD over the numbers of subsidized units that should be included in an annual HAP; and the Town's zoning provision prohibiting multi-family housing outside of Huntington Station had just been invalidated by the Court itself, and therefore would no longer be a factor.

I remain convinced that the appeals judges' extraordinary action was what eliminated—for nearly 40 years to this point—any possibility of housing construction outside of Huntington Station for the very people who had lent their names to the lawsuit. I know what a heady experience it can be to participate in a major "test case," but law can be made without hurting one's own clients.

Ralph told me that Bellman had adamantly insisted that his clients authorize him to press the Court to grant site-specific relief, over the objections of virtually everyone else participating in strategy discussions, including an NYU law professor recruited for the purpose, who thought that the request for that kind of relief would be "overreaching." Had I been on Bellman's side of the case, I would have agreed with the professor. But Bellman stuck to his guns and got what he wanted.

My usual confidence in my powers of persuasion was badly shaken. I felt that this was a case of great significance, with equities on both sides of the case, and that the Court should have resolved them in such a way that the parties could have accomplished their valid objectives and moved on. I hoped to win the case, but was prepared for the possibility of a loss, not, however, for a decision that I believed arose out of the judges' unjustified anger directed toward the town, and, I'm sorry to say, I did feel that their decision was "result-driven" and ideological.

I had further work to do. I was now faced with a difficult decision that involved making the same kind of political calculation that in my ideal world would not be part of legal strategic planning. The town could immediately file a direct appeal to the Supreme Court, or could ask the entire membership of judges on the Second Circuit to rehear the case, in what is called an *en banc* hearing. There were distinct advantages to the latter because several of the Circuit judges who would participate in a rehearing, unlike any of the judges on the original panel, came from suburban areas and thoroughly understood zoning law. So, if there were a rehearing by all of the judges, there was a good possibility that one or more would rule in favor of the town and be able to authoritatively lay out zoning precepts that the original panel ignored. That would have put us in a stronger position in the Supreme Court; instead of a unanimous three-judge opinion against us, there would probably have been one or more contrary opinions at the appeal court level that would carry considerable weight.

I discussed the options with Arlene Lindsay, Huntington's Town Attorney. It was very tempting to make the *en banc* motion but doing so would delay the Supreme Court's consideration of the matter for at least six months.

An unsolicited telephone call from the office of President Reagan's Solicitor General in Washington made the decision for us.

The case had attracted the attention of the conservative community. I was strongly urged to bypass the full Circuit Court. The Reagan administration's lawyers were alarmed by the panel's decision, and wanted the opportunity to ask the Supreme Court to reverse it. The presidential election was imminent, and there was a possibility, however slim, that Michael Dukakis, rather than George H. W. Bush, would be President by the time the appeal was heard. The views of a Dukakis Solicitor General would almost certainly be antagonistic to the town's position. I knew from the Bianchi case what a strong influence the "Tenth Justice" has upon the Supreme Court, and now I was now being told that the Solicitor General was strongly inclined to seek a reversal. Arlene and I decided that the interests of our client—the town—dictated that we pass on a second bite in the Second Circuit and file an immediate appeal. In so doing, I was facilitating the very kind of political intervention that I deplored.

It turned out badly. The Solicitor General looked at the briefs below and concluded that we did not adequately crystallize our "discriminatory intent" argument to preserve it for the Court's review. Doing what he could do to preserve the "discriminatory intent" argument for conservatives to fight for in a future case, the Solicitor General asked the Court to affirm our defeat on very narrow grounds, without reaching that key question.

The case came to an end on November 7, 1988, the day before Election Day, when George H. W. Bush won the Presidency despite the Solicitor General's fears. The Court summarily affirmed the Second Circuit's ruling that restricting apartments to the Huntington Station area violated the law because it had a discriminatory effect. Because of the technical way the Court reached that conclusion, its decision was not a nationwide stamp of approval for the "effects" test, and the fight was indeed preserved for another day.

It was some consolation that Justices White, Marshall and Stevens disagreed with the Court's summary disposition of the appeal, and voted to hear it in full. First of all, it indicated that at least three justices, contrary to the Solicitor General, concluded that we had indeed preserved the "intent" issue for the Court's review. Secondly, even though Justice Marshall would not have been sympathetic to the town's position, having all nine justices consider the case, and having the support of the Solicitor General on the merits of the case, would, in my judgment, have given us a fair shot at a reversal, or at least, a careful and thorough discussion of the wisdom and practicality of the "effects" test.

After these events, one of my friends at the bar told me, "tell me who your judges are in a case, and I'll tell you whether you'll win or lose. You drew three liberals." I came to believe he was right. Editorial writers and legal "experts" now habitually predict how the individual justices of the Supreme Court will vote on a case, and they base their predictions upon the political orientation of each. I don't like thinking that that is how judges decide cases and didn't like it then. But unfortunately they have a valid point. I'd like someday for it to be an invalid one, and that there is a way for the courts to decide "political" cases other than on the basis of partisan preference.

The question that I wanted decided in 1988, and that the Solicitor General initially said he wanted decided in the Town's favor, was left unresolved for 27 years. In 2015, Texas Department of Housing and Community Affairs v Inclusive Communities Project, Inc. came to the Court, which ruled that a Fair Housing Act violation may be proven by showing discriminatory effect; showing discriminatory intent is not necessary.

If the Supreme Court had tackled the merits of the case in 1988, it may have decided the principal legal question the same way, but if so, I imagine the opinion would have been far more satisfying than that of the Second Circuit. In the Inclusive Communities case, Justice Anthony Kennedy eloquently addressed the roots and evils of housing segregation, used the tools of statutory construction in comparing the language of the Fair Housing Act to that in other civil rights laws, and made, I thought, a far more compelling case for outlawing state and local laws that contributed to that kind of segregation, than had the Second Circuit so many years before.

In that case, the Supreme Court, in common with so many other courts through the years, made law, did so in measured fashion, and did no more than it should. It was no accident that that carefully-thought-out decision was crafted by Justice Kennedy, respected in his time for having the ability to respect the legitimacy of views that did not align with his prior political inclinations. He changed society's rules in such a way that those initially inclined to disagree with his conclusions were able to respect them and hopefully adapt to them.

But the Second Circuit's resolution of the legal question in Housing Help's favor did not solve its problems on the ground. As of this writing, construction of Matinecock Court has still not begun. The lot at the Elwood and Pulaski intersection remains empty and forlorn. In Marianne Garvin's words, "it was a great victory—but no housing was built."

That having been said, there was later litigation between the parties, also acrimonious, that contributed significantly to the delay. Housing Help claimed that the town was again violating the Fair Housing Act by continuing after 1988 to obstruct the development of the project by opposing state funding. Its new lawsuit against the town, together with a threat of further litigation by the U.S. Attorney's office, finally brought about a settlement allowing the project to proceed, but reducing the number of units from 162 to 155.

And it was recently reported that Suffolk County, despite receiving in late 2019 new petitions in opposition from a new group of East Northport residents, has now committed $2.4 million for infrastructure improvements for the Elwood-Pulaski property, completing the last of $66 million in commitments needed for Matinecock Court.

Perhaps now, after 40 years, Marianne Garvin's question will finally be answered.

I think it could have been answered better, a very long time ago.

10
CLIMATE CHANGE

Both major political parties and their adherents use the courts to change public policy. More often than not, the cases they bring are "political," because the issues involve the most important and sometimes the most intimate of subjects, about which large numbers of Americans care greatly, and disagree strongly. Elected officials ordinarily find it advantageous to showcase the alignment of their views with those of their political "base." If an issue is deemed sufficiently important to that "base," and resort to the legislative process seems unlikely to resolve it in the way the base prefers, a court case may be filed. And, politics being what it is in America, it may well be filed, if possible, at a time and in a place such that the final or definitive court to hear it will be dominated by judges whose perceived political views align with those of the filer. Deliberately submitting a case to a partisan judge or group of judges because they are partisan is clearly contrary to the stated ideals of the bar and of the justice system itself, both of which advocate for judicial independence; but it nonetheless happens in real life. To paraphrase Chief Justice John Roberts' comments on another subject, the only way we can uphold those ideals and avoid the selection of partisan judges may be to uphold those ideals and avoid the selection of partisan judges.

"Judge shopping" of the type I describe could not occur at all if there were no partisan judges on the bench to shop for; but that objective—although specifically intended by the founders—is unlikely of achievement. But we must make as strong an effort as we can to insure that judges, particularly if appointed as a reward for their political service, are not placed on the bench with the understanding, explicit or implicit, that they will continue in their rulings to favor the causes they fought for as politicians. The process and the standards by which they are selected set the stage for the way they will perform their duties, how they will see themselves, and how people will see them, during all the years of their career. Judges cannot retain the respect and deference that enable them to effectively perform their critical role, unless they are chosen in a transparent process, and, after being chosen, they are willing and able to fully put aside their political preferences and to be insulated from political influence during their service.

The founders knew that judicial independence was a critical necessity if the court system was to function properly. They recognized human frailty, expected abuses of power by the two political branches of government, and specifically designed the federal courts to be an independent check upon them, a function that judges cannot perform if they remain in thrall to political interests.

Successive American leaders, presidents, prominent members of the judiciary and leaders of the Bar, have emphasized the importance of the courts' making their decisions free of political or ideological influence. As recently as December 2019, Chief Justice Roberts delivered a pointed reminder that "a strong and independent judiciary" is a "key source of national unity and stability;" and that—

> [i]n our age, when social media can instantly spread rumor and false information on a grand scale, the public's need to understand our

> government, and the protections it provides, is vital. The judiciary has an important role to play in civic education ... Chief Justice Warren illustrated the power of a judicial decision as a teaching tool in Brown v Board of Education, the great school desegregation case. His unanimous opinion on the most pressing issue of the era was a mere 11 pages—short enough that newspapers could publish all or almost all of it and every citizen could understand the Court's rationale ... We should ... remember that justice is not inevitable. We should reflect on our duty to judge without fear or favor, deciding each matter with humility, integrity and dispatch....We should each resolve to do our best to maintain the public's trust that we are faithfully discharging our solemn obligation to equal justice under law.

President Eisenhower's 1955 address honored the "reputation for greatness" of Chief Justice John Marshall, who, he said—

> established himself, in character, in wisdom, and in his clear insights into the requirements of government, as a shining example for all later members of his profession ... He made of the Constitution a vital, dynamic, deathless charter for free and orderly living in the United States ... One result of his work was to create among Americans a deep feeling of trust and respect for the judiciary. Rarely indeed has that respect been damaged or that trust betrayed by the judicial branch of our three-sided government.

Eisenhower was so committed to a nonpartisan judiciary that he thought it was "obvious" that "a rough equality between the two great American political parties" should be maintained on the bench "to help assure that the judiciary will realistically appraise and apply precedent and principles in the light of current American thinking, and will never become a repository of unbalanced partisan attitudes."

That is neither a naive nor an unprecedented way of attempting to balance the judiciary. A number of independent federal agencies, which make quasi-judicial decisions, are required by law to have bipartisan membership, so there is no principled reason why we should not accord full-fledged judicial activities the same status. In fact, in New York for a number of years, a bipartisan effort was made to insure that each of the two major political parties would be represented on the federal bench.

Until now, the notion that the judiciary should be nonpartisan has rarely been openly challenged in America. During the years I practiced, it would have been unthinkable for a lawyer considered for elevation to the bench to declare that he or she placed a higher value upon loyalty to a political party than upon judicial independence.

Times have changed. We have "climate change" in America, but not only the type we have been reading about. Safeguards devised over two centuries to minimize political influence upon the courts are being dismantled, the independence of the judiciary is under direct and open attack, and the way people in high and low places today talk and even *think* about the courts is dramatically different from before. Judges are increasingly being seen as "politicians with robes."

It is regrettable that President Donald Trump actively promotes that change. He publicly demeans those he terms "so-called judges" if they render decisions that displease him. He issued a pardon to Arizona Sheriff Joe Arpaio, who was found guilty of criminal contempt for disobeying federal court orders directing him to cease targeting Latino drivers, an action that seemed to be based upon bias against Latinos.

The president's exercise of the pardon power appears to be based upon his view that the actions engaged in by the individuals he has pardoned should be encouraged rather than prosecuted. It also seems intended to circumvent the systems and structures that Americans have long depended upon to adjudicate difficult questions of guilt or innocence. He announced that he had pardoned three members of the armed forces convicted or accused of war crimes, saying that "when our soldiers have to fight for our country, I want to give them the confidence to fight," and his decision was widely criticized as undermining the military justice system and ignoring the rule of law. The *Washington Post* reported that Pentagon leaders were "fuming" about the president's intervention to "overrule military justice," and his action led to the departure of the Secretary of the Navy, who believed that it undercut the "good order and discipline" prized by the military. District of Columbia Federal Judge Paul L. Friedman condemned the president for "violating democratic norms," and the *New York Times* editorial board strongly protested his action, stating "the United States military—and its civilian commander—doesn't have the luxury of simply asserting that it is morally superior to its enemies. It needs to be morally superior, which means abiding by the rule of law."

It is in stark contrast to our professed views in this country, as well as a matter of broad concern, that leaders of nations "experiencing the rise of authoritarianism" consider it critical to their maintenance of power to undercut the independence of the courts. In 2017, China's Chief Justice Zhou Qiang, stated "We should resolutely resist erroneous influence from the West; 'constitutional democracy,' 'separation of powers' and 'independence of the judiciary'." That statement caused Jerome A. Cohen of the U.S.-Asia Law Institute of New York University, a long-time China scholar, to call Zhou's comments "the most enormous ideological setback for decades of halting, uneven progress toward the creation of a professional, impartial judiciary." Similar attacks upon an independent court system have been made by "strongmen" in Turkey, Hungary, and Poland, who "have taken their countries in authoritarian directions." Tolerance on our part for the politicization of our courts has a significant potential to take America, too, in an authoritarian direction.

There are many ways that the independence of the courts can be undermined. In America, in a number of states, "recall" laws have been enacted, allowing a judge to be unseated at any time during his or her statutory term of office if a petition with sufficient voter signatures places the question on the ballot. Judges have been removed from the bench for unpopular decisions. As of April 2018, it was reported that legislators in 16 states were considering 51 bills to diminish or politicize the judiciary's role. By the end of that year, ABA President Bob Carlson reported that those numbers had increased to 18 state legislatures and at least 60 bills which would politicize the judicial selection process by giving legislatures or governors more control over it, or "discourage independent decision-making" by increasing the likelihood of judges being impeached for unpopular decisions.

The federal courts have long operated under a random case assignment system, but there's a way of circumventing it: in judicial districts with multiple smaller divisions where as few as one or two judges may be assigned, lawyers filing cases in those divisions have at least a 50-50 chance of getting a judge they believe has views sympathetic to their clients.

RICHARD C. CAHN

A widely-condemned act by another political leader made a major contribution to the politicization of our highest Court. Majority Leader Mitch McConnell's refusal to allow the Senate to consider the nomination of Merrick Garland to the Court was an outright abandonment of the rule of law: the Senate refused to perform its constitutional duty to consider the confirmation of all duly nominated judges, and left the Supreme Court one member short for nearly a year. McConnell's decision cannot be seen as a principled or nonpartisan one; he made it known that if a Court vacancy should occur during the last year of President Trump's first term, he would press forward with Senate confirmation of any replacement. There should be a standing rule of the Senate requiring prompt consideration of appointments submitted by the president at any time during his or her term in office; and a full Senate vote should quickly follow.

It is a devastating blow to the courts' independence that federal judicial selection has become a nakedly partisan process. For many years, it was focused solely upon "the professional competence, integrity and judicial temperament of each nominee."

Dating from the Eisenhower years, the American Bar Association's Standing Committee on the Judiciary, using those criteria, reviewed candidates for the federal courts, and except for the George W. Bush administration, screening took place prior to a candidate's formal nomination. Most presidents, regardless of party affiliation, quietly abandoned nominations of candidates who did not receive a "well-qualified" or "qualified" rating from the ABA.

In New York, good-faith efforts were made to reduce the role of political affiliation and divide federal judicial appointments between the major political parties. The White House usually appointed candidates recommended by screening committees set up by each of the state's two senators. If those senators were from different political parties, the judgeships were divided, three for the

MAKING LAW

senator aligned with the president's party and one for the senator aligned with the other.

For a long period of time, the Senate would not proceed with any confirmation without the approval of both senators from the nominee's state, which they signified by handing in a "blue slip." Whatever their political affiliation, senators most likely to be familiar with a candidate's work and reputation played a critical role at the beginning of the confirmation process.

Today, many senators no longer have active judicial screening committees. Majority Leader McConnell ended the "blue slip" practice. Time allotted for Senate floor debate on judicial nominations, formerly as much as 20 or 30 hours, is now as little as two hours. In 2017, the Trump administration downgraded the role of the ABA, announcing that it would no longer permit review of candidates' qualifications in advance of nomination, and pressed forward with judicial candidates whom the ABA rated "unqualified," a number of whom were confirmed and are now on the bench for life.

The Trump administration now nominates candidates for federal judgeships who, the president openly admits, have been "picked by the Federalist Society," an organization which makes ideological credentials "central to the nominating process." Candidates for all levels of the federal judiciary, including the Supreme Court, come from lists compiled by Leonard Leo, the organization's executive vice president. In this way, the president has outsourced one of his most consequential decisions to a partisan political organization, and the candidates that it puts forward—Justices Neil Gorsuch and Brett Kavanagh are examples—have often long been faithful adherents to its views.

In short, Eisenhower-era procedures have been effectively abandoned, and the process that has now been substituted will not produce judges who will be, or be seen by the public to be, independent of political bias.

RICHARD C. CAHN

Having served on two judicial screening committees, I know that it is often difficult, if not impossible, to know with confidence whether a candidate is too strongly wedded to a partisan political point of view to cast it aside after becoming a judge; but such candidates may now be the only ones interviewed. As Justice Anthony Kennedy pointed out, without neutrality the courts lose public respect and hence allegiance.

Loss of neutrality is now a clear and present danger. If the present trends continue, the justice system will soon be fully politicized, unless the public understands the significance of what is happening and is willing to take necessary steps to stop it.

Americans are willing to bring to the courts difficult disputes of all kinds—including controversial "political" questions such as abortion, gun rights, school prayer and civil rights protections—and abide by the results. That indicates a generally shared view that most judges are impartial, but that view will become untenable if judges routinely shape the law to fit their own ideological mold. "Political" cases are obviously not the only ones requiring judges to be impartial and independent. Every private litigant in the court system also expects and is entitled to fairness and impartiality. But in the "political question" cases, and in the overlapping group of cases raising classic abuse of power claims that Hamilton intended the courts to review, a judge's ideology is most likely to skew the result.

It is essential that we restore and improve upon our prior non-partisan judicial selection procedures and our institutional protections to insulate sitting judges from political influence. Only in that way can we ensure—and we must ensure—that the judiciary never becomes "a repository of unbalanced partisan attitudes."

If we do not, our democracy will not likely survive.

And that is—and should be—a matter of urgent concern to us all.

ACKNOWLEDGMENTS

I'd like to acknowledge those who inspired me to embark on this project.

Four judges I've previously mentioned, who because of the high esteem I have for them and their work, provided a good part of my writing inspiration, although neither they nor I were thinking then that there would ever be one: Federal Judges Algernon Butler and Charles P. Sifton, and New York Court of Appeals Judge Stanley Fuld and Chief Judge Judith Kaye. They were two Republicans and two Democrats, and they showed that neither political party has a monopoly on good judges. They loved the law and were dedicated to keeping it relevant and fair.

Several lawyers deserve mention here. All of them recognized the special nature of our mission as lawyers and embraced the duty of candor and honesty that their licenses imposed upon them. Although except in one case they represented clients whose interests were not aligned with the interests of mine, we found ourselves acting cooperatively to bring about a fair result that each of us could be proud of. Assistant U.S. Attorney Bob Begleiter and U.S. Attorney Thomas McNamara were nominal adversaries. Assistant Solicitor General Francis Beytagh, April Charney, and Lewis Silverman represented third parties. Sanford Levine,

RICHARD C. CAHN

Counsel for the State University of New York, and I were representing the same client in the Baby Jane Doe case, but he is among the lawyers I particularly admire for his idealism, and in the litigation context, for his ability to balance his passion with good, plain lawyering. And I should not neglect Fred Block, who, by conceiving of the Bianchi case, more than redeemed himself from making all those late-at-night telephone calls; his idea placed me at the center of a fabulous adventure.

I've mentioned Fred Rodell, my favorite professor at Yale Law School, several times. Fred taught me to look deeply into what was really happening in the courts, rather than what the law books claimed were happening. I didn't subscribe to all of Fred's views, but in a way my other mentors did not, he forced me to realize that what I did as a trial lawyer would not just make a difference to the development of the law—a satisfying accomplishment in itself—but that it would (or should) directly affect real people in the real world, which was far more important. His lesson came back to me forcefully when Marianne Garvin gave me her identical "take" on Housing Help's strategy in the NAACP case.

There were a number of individuals who shared their recollections with me as I tried to reconstruct the details of all of these cases: Bob Stevenson, Colette MacDonald's brother and the uncle of Kimberly and Kristen MacDonald, helped me know the members of the Kassab-Stevenson family both before and after the murders far better than I did when I was representing them. Tom McNamara, the North Carolina U.S. Attorney, was the public defender for North Carolina's eastern district when I spoke to him in recent years, and he gave me some of the back story, including his interactions with Judge Butler after my phone call with him in April 1974, and how Butler reacted to the presentation we made to him. Brian Murtagh, the highly-skilled and indefatigable Army lawyer, spent virtually all of his professional career on the MacDonald case, and filled in many gaps in my knowledge of the evidence and the personalities in the case. He also went through the draft of my Touro Law Review article reviewing Errol Morris's book, and kept me honest. My former secretary Barbara Pedersen helped me relive the preparation of the legal papers in the MacDonald case. Bob Armstrong, with whom I shared years as young lawyers in Huntington, moved in mid-life to practice law in Virginia, and his insights and experience as a former JAG lawyer, and later as a civilian lawyer handling cases in the military justice system, gave me a crash course in the disciplinary and honor codes at the service academies. Bob died in 2014, and the tributes that poured in were, as I would have expected, heartfelt eulogies to a warm, gentle, and fair man, who, in the words of one friend, "fought for justice right to the very end."

Lew Silverman and Mark Cohen filled me in on the hearings and the proceedings in the Baby Jane Doe case, and the opinions of the actors. And Margaret Levine, Sandy Levine's widow, told me how Sandy brought the Hudson River Club into the modern age by forcing it to accept women as members.

Marianne Garvin was exceedingly generous with her recollections about the NAACP case. During my single extended telephone conversation with Bob Ralph, even though he elected later not to continue it, he was very helpful and informative about the views of Housing Help's board members, and the organization's strategy decisions in the case.

I shared many reminiscences and details of the "triple murder" case with my former co-counsel Lenny Wexler, who served many years on the federal bench until his death in 2018.

The West Point Freedom of Information Office and the Academy's archives custodian, helped me reconstruct the evolution of the West Point disciplinary code as the Academy became co-educational in 1976.

RICHARD C. CAHN

Jane LaCova, who has served as the Executive Secretary of the Suffolk County Bar Association since before I became its President, has always been a tireless worker for an organization of great prestige and influence. At my request, she researched the association's archives and contributed material that enriched this manuscript, for which, in addition to the help she gave me during my year as president, I am grateful.

Dear friends of mine looked at parts of this manuscript. Mike Plumer has written his own story and has provided many valuable writing and organizational suggestions; Lois Stein gave me creative ideas about how to improve the presentation of the events detailed in the book; Marcia and Myron Stein contributed valuable perspective, Marcia, for many years the Executive Director of New York City's Meals on Wheels, knows first hand how those in the giving occupations learn to effectively interact with politicians; and Myron, a keen lawyer who in the earliest part of his legal career served as a clerk to a federal judge in the Southern District of New York. My friend, Bob Keeler, former *Newsday* reporter and member of the newspaper's editorial board, and I shared many hours reminiscing about the MacDonald case, and he generously undertook to edit a chapter of this book. Les Paldy, who knows far more than I do about how politics, academic life, and government service intersect, Mark Smoller, who writes on deadline every month, and Ron Lazar, who always has common sense on his side, could not have encouraged me more to complete and publish this work.

And above all, there was my family: My loyal wife, Vivian, refrained from complaining when I spent hours working on this manuscript on my computer, read an interminable number of drafts, sharpened my thinking and approach, and immeasurably improved the resulting manuscript. My daughter Lisa, who is a producer and director of audio books, quickly crystallized ideas that I was struggling to articulate. And I've been quietly cheered on by my son Dan, the third generation to practice law under the name Cahn & Cahn, who has always wanted to know more about "what it was like in the olden days."

The germ of the idea for this book came out of a conversation I had many years ago with my oldest Irish grandson, Eli, then about 10, as we built a sand castle on the beach at Galway Bay. I realized that neither he nor his three Dublin-born siblings, Rosa, Sammy and Finn, would ever know what their grandfather did all his life across the Great Pond unless I wrote it down. I later realized that my all-American grandchildren, Ash, Andrew, Ava and Jack, who live here, were just as unlikely to know what happened in those years before they were born, unless I recorded it for them, too. And so I have, for all of them.

I tip my hat to Eli for another reason: for many years we shared the joys and agonies of writing. During those years, following Ireland's superb literary tradition, he was turning his interest and talent into *Green Fire*, a beautifully-conceived and carefully crafted novel, beating me to publication by a full year in the process.

I am also grateful to a small number of people who spoke to me "off the record" about important things that occurred behind some of the scenes I described. All of them helped me to recapture and hopefully accurately describe, the events I have written about, in a way I could not have done alone, and kept me from making more factual mistakes than I have probably done anyway. They know who they are, and I thank them here.

NOTES

Page 16 ...*I researched the question decades later*... What I discovered turned out to be a fascinating back story, that I published for the Dartmouth Alumni Magazine in July 2016.

Pages 16-17...*Don't Join the Bookburners*"... https://dartmouthalumnimagazine.com/articles/"don't-join-book-burners", last accessed January 8, 2020

Page 18 ..."*to the very end [Rodell] was joyously unrepentant*"... Wright, Goodbye to Fred Rodell, 89 Yale L J No. 8 (July 1980) at 1456.

Page 19 ...*Seeger politely told them*... https://www.latimes.com/opinion/la-xpm-2014-jan-29-la-ol-pete-seeger-1955-huac-hearing-20140129-story.html, last accessed January 8, 2020

Page 24 ...*Lord Herschell made plain*...The citation of Palmer v Wick is (1894) AC 318, 324

Page 25 ...*the rule would not change. Not yet* ... The Dole case is reported at 30 NY 2d 143 (1972). Three years before Dole was decided, the Berg case came to a happy ending as far as the town was concerned, when the Appellate Division dismissed all claims against it, finding that the facts "demonstrated that the sole proximate cause of the accident was the manner in which the automobile was being operated." Berg v. Town of Huntington, 295 NYS 2d 1004 (2d Dept. 1969).

Page 34 ... *written about "mental coercion"*... Joost A. M. Meerloo, "The Rape of the Mind," World Publishing Company, 1956.

Page 42 ...*A single judge can stop the President*... See Morris, "Leadership on the Federal Bench: The Craft and Activism of Jack Weinstein," Oxford University Press (2011) at 23 ("through equitable remedies, judges can impose policy judgments on administrators and elected officials...their decisions resolve disputes, enforce norms, and allocate social values.") This is so well accepted that the debate within the legal profession has now moved on to questioning whether it is appropriate in a case involving one region of the country to issue an injunction preventing the federal government from carrying out a challenged policy anywhere in the nation. Katie Benner, *"A DACA Question: Should Judges Use Local Cases to Halt National Orders?"* New York Times, January 14, 2018 at p. 14. Recently, the Trump administration has decided to challenge the practice directly.

Pages 42 ...*No party appears in the federal court dockets more than the federal government* ... Morris, "Leadership on the Federal Bench: The Craft and Activism of Jack Weinstein," Oxford University Press (2011) at 1. Morris also points out that "the federal district courts are very much a part of the American political process [but] the federal courts have come to do more than this...[they] attempt to assure equal treatment and governmental 'fair play,' keeping agencies within their constitutional and statutory limits."

Page 43. .... *Supreme Court decisions in recent times*... In *Engel v Vitale*, 370 U.S. 421 (1962), the Supreme Court outlawed prayer in public schools. In *District of Columbia v. Heller*, 554 U.S. 570 (2008), the Court invalidated certain District of Columbia restrictions applicable to guns in the home, and ruled that the Second Amendment protected an individual's right to bear arms, without regard to whether that individual is a member of a "militia" or not. In *Burwell v. Hobby Lobby*, 1345 S. Ct. 2751 (2014), business owners, citing their strongly-held religious beliefs, challenged the government's requirement that their company was required in certain ways to provide or facilitate the provision of contraceptive coverage in the company's employee health insurance plan. The Supreme Court found that a business could lawfully refuse on the basis of its owners' First Amendment religious beliefs to provide contraceptive coverage in connection with the health plan it made available to its employees, or to cooperate in notifying the health care provider of its decision, so as to enable the provider to arrange for such coverage through a government program. In *Citizens United v. FEC*, 558 U.S. 310 (2010), a nonprofit corporation that had produced for television a video attacking Hillary Clinton's fitness for office, successfully sued the Federal Election Commission, the Court declaring that the federal law prohibiting a corporation or union from expending its funds for an "electioneering communication" advocating the election or defeat of a candidate within 30 day of a primary election, violated the First Amendment's guarantee of free speech. In *Shelby County v Holder*, 570 U.S. 529 (2013), the Supreme Court eliminated the "preclearance" provisions of the Voting Rights Act of 1964.

Page 45… *delivered an earlier address* … Eisenhower's 1955 speech was to the American Bar Association. http://tucnak.fsv.cuni.cz/~calda/Documents/1950s/Ike_Geneva_55.html, last accessed March 25, 2020.

Page 45 …. *future Justice Neil Gorsuch published* ….Gorsuch, Liberals'N'Lawsuits, found at https://www.nationalreview.com/2005/02/liberalsnlawauites - joseph-4, last accessed June 10, 2019. In the article, Gorsuch quoted David von Drehle, a Washington Post columnist and "self-identified liberal," as recognizing "that American liberals have become addicted to the courtroom, relying on judges and lawyers, rather than elected leaders and the ballot box, as the primary means of effecting their social agenda."

Pages 45-46 ...*George F. Will regrets* ... Will, in "The Conservative Sensibility" (Hachette Books, 2019) strongly supports judicial review of governmental actions. At page 192, he says "...the lesson of 206 years of constitutional history is, alas, clear: If the federal government is to be limited, it will be limited not by congressional or presidential devotions to constitutional niceties, but only by properly engaged courts diligently construing the Constitution. Absent such judicial engagement, the Constitution will be merely a parchment barrier to enlargements of the federal government's sphere." At page 199-201, he says "courts matter in America more than in any other democracy."... "[I]t ... is elementary that not all injustices are created equal, and those that violate important rights must, for that reason, be declared illegitimate. Declared by whom? By the non-majoritarian portion of government, the judiciary.... So it falls to judicial supervision of democracy to help preserve the institutional equilibrium." At p. 205-207, Will agrees with Timothy Sandefur's criticism of conservatives' "indiscriminate denunciations of 'judicial activism'," saying that "[t]he protection of rights, those constitutionally enumerated and others, requires a judiciary actively engaged in enforcing what the Constitution actually is 'basically about', which is compelling majority power to respect individuals' rights." Will affirms the "judicial duty to police the excesses of majorities," agreeing with a Texas Judge, Don Willett, that "There must remain judicially enforceable constraints on legislative actions that are irreconcilable with constitutional commands." Will adopts Willett's description of the "profound difference between an activist judge and an engaged judge:" Will's formulation is "The former creates rights that are neither specified in nor implied by

MAKING LAW

the Constitution. The latter defends rights the Framers actually placed there — and the unenumerated rights they acknowledged — and prevents the elected branches from usurping the judiciary's duty to declare what the Constitution means." And finally, at p. 213, he concludes that "for many years and for several reasons, too many conservatives have unreflectively and imprudently celebrated 'judicial restraint'."
The quotes in this footnote and the text are from The Conservative Sensibility by George F. Will, copyright © 2019, 2020. Reprinted by permission of Hachette Books, an imprint of Hachette Book Group, Inc.

Page 46… *enough judges and lawyers took the professional rules and traditions seriously…* David Brooks has written movingly about this, The Lawyers Who Would Not Break: The U.S. Legal system is Withstanding the Trump Onslaught, New York Times, February 22, 2019, at p. A-27. Writing about Robert Khuzami, the Deputy U.S. Attorney in the Southern District of New York, Brooks wrote: "He's part of a team. There are teams like that spread anonymously throughout the U.S. government. They are clinging tenaciously to the old standards of right and wrong, to the Constitution and the rule of law."

Page 46…*Justice Anthony Kennedy put it this way…* The quote is from a "Frontline" interview aired in 1999 on PBS. Available at https://www.pbs.org/wgbh/pages/frontline/shows/justice/interviews/supremo.html, last accessed September 24, 2019.

Page 48 …*rely heavily on intuition and also on emotion…* Richard Posner, "How Judges Think," Harvard University Press (2008), at 112.

Pages 48-49 …*much earlier, Benjamin Cardozo…* Lectures, "The Nature of the Judicial Process," Yale University Press, 1921.

Page 50 …*Rule 3.1. of the American Bar Association's Model Rules* … The Rule, entitled "Meritorious Claims and Contentions, reads in pertinent part: "A lawyer shall not bring or defend a proceeding, or assert or controvert an issue therein, unless there is a basis in law and fact for doing so that is not frivolous, which includes a good faith argument for an extension, modification or reversal of existing law."

https://www.americanbar.org/groups/professional_responsibility/publications/model_rules_of_professional_conduct/rule_3_1_meritorious_claims_contentions/, last accessed September 24, 2019.

Page 68 ...*recognize that their integrity, and that of their office*... Begleiter was highly respected by his colleagues in the U.S. Attorney's office, and several years after the West Point case, he was promoted to Chief of the Civil Division, and served in that position for seven years.

Page 69 .... *Second Circuit dismissed a case, Doe v. Hagenbeck*.... The case can be found at 870 F. 3d 36 (2d Cir. 2017).

Pages 69 .... *promoted a sexually aggressive culture*... 870 F. 3d 36, 38 (2d Cir. 2017).

Page 70....*she was simply a student* ... Doe v. Hagenbeck, 870 F. 3d 36, 51 (2d Cir. 2017) (Chen, J., dissenting).

Page 70... *even a 1983 Supreme Court decision* ... The case was Chappell v. Wallace, 462 U.S. 296 (1983), which held that there was a need to insulate the military's disciplinary structure from judicial inquiry unless "special factors" were present.

Page 74 ....*parents were blindsided*. Marcia Chambers, "Baby Doe: Hard Case for Parents and Courts," New York Times, January 8, 1984.

Page 80 ...*the appeals court unanimously overruled*...The Appellate Division decision is Weber v. Stony Brook Hospital, 95 AD 2d 587 (2d Dept. 1983). The New York Court of Appeals affirmance can be found at 60 NY 2d 208 (1983).

Page 83 ...*Wexler quickly dismissed the government's arguments* ... United States v. University Hospital, 575 F. Supp. 607 (1983).

MAKING LAW

Page 85 ....*sued the government, challenging*... Bowen v. American Hospital Association, 476 US 610, 647 (1986).

Page 87 ....*and Friday night she returned to be with her parents*... Nicole Fuller, "Baby Jane Doe at 30: Happy, joking, learning," Newsday, October 13, 2013.

Page 88 ...*Baker v. Carr*... The citation of the case is 369 U.S.186 (1962).

Page 111. .... *I think we shall finally succeed*... Webster correctly predicted the result, as the Supreme Court rejected New Hampshire's effort to invalidate the College Charter. Trustees of Dartmouth College v. Woodward, 17 U.S. 518 (1819).

Page 114 ....*skew political results*..."Creating unequally populous districts is not, however, the only way to skew political results by setting district lines. The choice to draw a district line one way, not another, always carries some consequence for politics, save in a mythical State with voters of every political identity distributed in an absolutely gray uniformity. The spectrum of opportunity runs from cracking a group into impotent fractions, to packing its members into one district for the sake of marginalizing them in another. However equal districts may be in population as a formal matter, the consequence of a vote cast can be minimized or maximized, and if unfairness is sufficiently demonstrable, the guarantee of equal protection condemns it as a denial of substantial equality." *Vieth v. Jubelirer*, 541 U.S. 267, 343 (2004), Souter, J., dissenting.

Page 114 ...*sequels to the reapportionment cases of the 1960's, came to the Court*... In *Gill v Whitford*, the Circuit Court had ruled that a redistricting plan enacted by the Wisconsin Legislature in 2011, "constitutes an unconstitutional gerrymander." By a 2-1 vote, it held that the act "was intended to burden the rights of the Democratic voters throughout the decennial period by impeding their ability to translate their votes into legislative seats," and found that the plan was neither "explained by the political geography of Wisconsin, nor is it justified by a legitimate state interest." The Supreme Court declined to rule on the merits, and remitted that case to the lower courts for further proceedings. In *Benisek v Lamone*, involving Maryland, the lower court had ruled that Plaintiffs were not entitled to a preliminary injunction preventing a new districting plan from operating in the 2018 election cycle. The plaintiffs alleged that the Democratic-controlled state legislature had violated their First Amendment rights by retaliating against them for their support of a Republican candidate in the State's Sixth Congressional district. The alleged retaliation consisted of the gerrymandering of that district's lines, resulting in the dilution of the Republican vote in the district, which dropped from 47% to 33%. The Supreme Court declined to rule on the merits in this case as well, holding that the case should have been heard by a three-judge court, and returned this case, like the Wisconsin one, to the lower courts.

Page 114 … *"incompatible" with democratic principles*… The citations are from Chief Justice Roberts' opinion in Rucho v. Common Cause, 138 S. Ct. 2679 (2019), decided June 27, 2019. The holding that gerrymandering cases represented "political questions" beyond the jurisdiction of the federal courts stood in stark contrast with the Court's 1962 decision in Baker v. Carr. Justice Kagan's dissent directly challenged the majority's conclusion, saying that checking partisan gerrymandering is "*not* beyond the courts, that courts around the country "have coalesced around manageable judicial standards" and that the standards used in the cases before the Court allow "judicial intervention in the worst-of-the-worst cases of democratic subversion, causing blatant constitutional harms." In "giving such gerrymanders a pass from judicial review, she said the majority of the Court "goes tragically wrong."

Page 123 ...*was contrived and false....* I wrote a review of "*A Wilderness of Error,*" by Errol Morris, in which he selectively reviewed the evidence that was used to convict Jeffrey MacDonald of the murders of his wife and daughters, concluding that the prosecution was flawed and that MacDonald was deprived of a fair trial. I found his book provocative but unpersuasive. Some of the material in this chapter is taken from that review in the Touro Law Review, Volume 29, Number 1, at p. 75 (2012).

Page 125 ....*the proverbial dog that did not bark...* This wonderful imagery comes from Arthur Conan Doyle's 1892 story, "The *Adventure of Silver Blaze.*"

Page 126 ....*you die a little in the process....* Fred Kassab, *Vendetta* (1979) (unpublished manuscript in the author's possession) and also available at http://www.thejeffreymacdonaldcase.com/html/kassab_vendetta.html.

Page 130 ....*close even if we couldn't say a word....* Fred Kassab, *Vendetta*, referenced at page 126.

Page 131 ...*The fight started with my first meeting in Raleigh....*Fred Kassab, *How it All Started,* (unpublished manuscript in the author's possession).

Page 139 ... *he discussed the matter extensively with McNamara and two days later with Weldon Hollowell* ... handwritten notes of Hon. Algernon Butler, Chief Judge, U.S. District Court, Eastern District of North Carolina, from the library of the University of North Carolina, Algernon Butler collection, and used by its permission.

Pages 144-145 ...Dear Mr. Attorney General... letter from Chief Judge Algernon Butler to Hon. William Saxbe, Attorney General of the United States, dated May 1, 1974, copy in author's possession.

Page 152... *a variety of recently invented and difficult to understand financial instruments...for* a thoroughly readable account of the financial crisis, I refer you to Michael Lewis, "The Big Short: The Doomsday Machine," Norton, 2010.

Page 154 ... *to record documents that misrepresented*....There was another serious defect in these mortgage instruments: in contradiction to the language that termed MERS the mortgagee, it also designated MERS as the "nominee" for the not yet designated "successors and assigns" of the original lender. This violates New York law, which requires "nominees" or "agents" to specifically identify the person or entity for which the agent will be acting. However, MERS' business plan depends upon this blanket designation, for without it, MERS could only lawfully transfer ownership of the mortgage once, on behalf of the original lender that had named MERS as its agent, to a new owner. Without specifically identifying that new owner, or the many successive owners, my view was that MERS had no authority to act for any of them. During the enormous "robo-signing" scandal, a wide array of individuals – some designating themselves as MERS vice presidents -- claimed, under oath, that they had examined the paperwork and could certify to a court that MERS had the authority to commence a proceeding to foreclose the mortgage at issue. Eventually, the Courts realized that many of these certifications were false or unreliable.

Page 154 .... *created by Congress for the purpose of increasing the availability of mortgage money*... The directives from Congress to both Fannie and Freddie were to "provide stability in the secondary market, increase liquidity, and access to mortgage credit across the nation". Hunter, "Government Sponsored Enterprises – Unfair Advantages or Safety Net?" Villanova University, 2001, available at http://www.learningace.com/doc/2567409/324646d8c4f343c64bfb93963c7ff67c/the-secondary-mortgage-market-whitney-hunter. See, also,

MAKING LAW

Brief for Amicus Curiae Mortgage Bankers Association at 8 et seq, *Merscorp, Inc., v. Romaine*, at 3, New York Court of Appeals, August 31, 2006.

Page 155 ....*you can point to no single case*...Transcript of May 15, 2001 argument, Record on Appeal at 1370, *Merscorp, Inc. v. Romaine*, 8 NY 3d 90 (2006).

Page 156 ....*register every mortgage loan in the United States*....Record on Appeal at 513, *Merscorp, Inc. v. Romaine*, 8 NY 3d 90 (2006).

Page 156 .... *Absolutely not*.... Transcript of deposition of Mark Fleming, Record on Appeal at 713, *Merscorp, Inc. v. Roma*ine, 8 NY 3d 90 (2006).

Page 157 ....*the most solid investment on the globe*.... Transcript of deposition of R. K. Arnold, at 144. *Merscorp, Inc. v. Romaine*, 8 NY 3d 90 (2006).

Page 157 ....*loan the money again to a new consumer*.... Transcript of deposition of R. K. Arnold, Record on Appeal at 592-593, *Merscorp, Inc. v. Romaine*, 8 NY 3d 90 (2006). The New York Times quoted an employee of Bear Stearns, a firm heavily into mortgage securitization, as saying, according to court documents, that "the loans were quickly sold to investors... We are a moving company, not a storage company." "E-Mails Suggest J.P. Morgan Hid Flaws in Some Loans", *New York Times*, February 7, 2013, page B1.

Page 157 ...*the University of Cincinnati Law Review would publish*...... "Foreclosure, Subprime Mortgage Lending, and the Mortgage Electronic Recording System", 78 University of Cincinnati Law Review, No. 4, Summer 2010, at p. 1407.

Page 158 ....*all founded on this little note and mortgage*.... Transcript of May 15, 2001 oral argument, Record on Appeal at 1358, *Merscorp, Inc. v. Romaine*, 8 NY 3d 90 (2006).

Page 158 ....*the public has no significant interest*... Record on Appeal at 731, *Merscorp, Inc. v. Romaine*, 8 NY 3d 90 (2006).

RICHARD C. CAHN

Pages 161-162 ....*without any negative effect on the rights of any parties*.... Brief for Amici Curiae Federal National Mortgage Association and Federal Home Loan Mortgage Association, *Merscorp, Inc., v. Romaine*, at 3, New York Court of Appeals, August 31, 2006.

Page 162... *the government takeover of Fannie and Freddie*... Between them, the two GSE's, had owned nearly a trillion dollars in mortgage-backed securities. Cummings and DiPasquale, City Research, "A Primer on the Secondary Mortgage Market," National Community Development Initiative Meetings, New York, NY, June 4, 1997, at p. 6.

Page 163 ....*extremely difficult to track exactly which lenders have claims to a home*....Gretchen Morgenson, *"Flawed Paperwork Aggravates a Foreclosure Crisis." New York Times*, October 4, 2010 at p. A1.

Page 164 ... *it was an important cog in the machine...incompletely documented mortgages that were destined for foreclosure*.... *"Foreclosure, Subprime Mortgage Lending, and the Mortgage Electronic Recording System"*, 78 University of Cincinnati Law Review, No. 4, Summer 2010, at p. 1407.

Page 164 ....*The Magic of the Mortgage Electronic Recording System: It is and it Isn't*.... David P. Weber, 85 American Bankruptcy Law Journal 239, Summer, 2011.

Page 165 ...*MERS began to "advise" its members to record mortgage transfers in county records, after all*.... Michael Powell and Gretchen Morgenson, MERS? It May Have Swallowed Your Loan, *New York Times*, March 6, 2011, Section BU, Page 1.

Page 165 ....*a six-year-old investigation of Fannie Mae and MERS*.... Gretchen Morgenson, A Mortgage Tornado Warning, Unheeded, *New York Times*, February 5, 2012, Section BU, Page 1.

Page 165 ....*the greatest failure of lawyering* .... Gretchen Morgenson, A Mortgage Tornado Warning, Unheeded, *New York Times*, February 5, 2012, Section BU, Page 1.

MAKING LAW

Page 166 ....*useless by masking beneficial ownership...Merscorp, Inc., v. Romaine*, 8 NY 3d at 104, New York Court of Appeals, August 31, 2006 (Kaye, C.J. dissenting).

Page 166 ....*arguably detract from the amount of public data available* .... *Merscorp, Inc., v. Romaine*, 8 NY 3d at 100, New York Court of Appeals, August 31, 2006 (Ciparek, J. concurring).

Page 166 ...*encouraging predatory lending practices... Merscorp, Inc., v. Romaine*, 8 NY 3d at 100, New York Court of Appeals, August 31, 2006 (Ciparek, J. concurring).

Pages 166-167 ... *"prepayment" sums that had been paid into MERS in one year*.... Record on Appeal at 625, *Merscorp, Inc. v. Romaine*, 8 NY 3d 90 (2006).

Page 167 ....*identify the current owner of the mortgage* .... mersinc.org, accessed February 14, 2018.

Page 167 ....*the "IOU" that a borrower signs... Bank of New York v. Silverberg*, 86 AD 3d 274, 926 NYS 2d 532 (2d Dept. 2011).

Page 178 ...*the Bethel AME Church*... *see*, Town of Huntington website, at https://huntingtonny.gov/filestorage/13747/99540/16499/Bethel_A.M.E._Church.pdf, last accessed January 12, 2020.

Page 181 ....*knocked down 250 dwellings and replaced them*.... Andrew Wiesz, "Places of their Own," University of Chicago Press (2004), at p. 107.

Page 182 .... *$7,000,000 of community development funds*....Nationally, Urban Renewal was replaced in 1974 by the Community Development Program, in which the federal government made a "block grant" to a state, which would then distribute the funds to local communities for programs similar to the earlier urban renewal activities. Huntington was the recipient of substantial funds from both the urban renewal and community development programs.

Page 196 ....*the Second Circuit judges determined* ... A scholarly journal later faulted the Second Circuit's analysis of discriminatory effect, pointing out that it "does not ensure that remedies to exclusionary zoning will actually result in the racial integration envisioned by the authors of the Fair Housing Act, rather than simply greater housing opportunities for low-income whites." Gordon, "Making Exclusionary Zoning Remedies Work: How Courts Applying Title VII Standards to Fair Housing Cases Have Misunderstood the Housing Market", 24 Yale Law & Policy Review (2006), 436, 468.

Pages 196-197..... *used those same numbers and came to opposite conclusions* .... *Huntington Branch, NAACP v. Town of Huntington, N.Y.,* 668 F. Supp. 762, 785 (EDNY, 1987); *Huntington Branch, NAACP v. Town of Huntington, N.Y.,* 844 F. 2d. 926, 938, (2d Cir. 1988).

Page 199 ....*stuck to his guns and got what he wanted*.... According to Ralph, shortly before the trial Bellman "mooted" the case, presenting his witnesses and strategy to an NYU law professor. The professor and virtually everyone else on the Plaintiffs' team disagreed with Bellman's plan to ask the Court to direct a specific rezoning of the property, feeling that taking such an aggressive approach would be "overreaching." Bellman steadfastly adhered to his position, and the appeals court did what he had asked, which in my view eliminated the any possibility of compromise of the case that could have led to the construction of low-income housing. My last hope to eliminate that part of the Second Circuit's decision was extinguished when the Supreme Court, which I believe would have had a difficult time affirming it, simply declined to review it.

Page 201 ....*concluded that we did not adequately crystallize*...While we argued in the lower courts that the zoning code's failure to affirmatively provide for privately-constructed apartments outside of Huntington Station, should be studied for "discriminatory effect," we also pointed out that the courts so far had also made it clear that some showing of discriminatory intent on the part of the local officials had to be made in order to establish a Fair

Housing Act violation. In our case, Judge Glasser's ruling that there was no proof "that enactment or implementation of the zoning code [was] motivated by discriminatory impulses" was not disturbed by the Second Circuit, and had our view of the requirements of the Fair Housing Act been adopted, that finding would have disposed of the case.

Page 202 ....*Texas Department of Housing & Community Affairs* ... The case is reported at 135 S. Ct. 2507 (2015).

Page 204... *To paraphrase Chief Justice John Roberts' comments*...In Parents Involved in Community Schools v. Seattle School District No. 1, 551 U.S. 701, 748 (2007), Chief Justice Roberts said, "The way to stop discrimination on the basis of race is to stop discriminating on the basis of race."

Page 207 ... *agencies, which make quasi-judicial decisions*...*See, for example*, Federal Election Commission v. Democratic Senatorial Campaign Committee, 454 U.S. 27, 37 (1981): "[T]he Commission is inherently bipartisan in that no more than three of its six voting members may be of the same political party."

Pages 207....*"so-called judges"*... "Trump Lashes Out at 'So-called' Judge Who Revoked his Travel Ban," https://www.politico.com/story/2017/02/trump-judge-james-robart-234645, last accessed April 9, 2018; "Trump Takes Up G.O.P. Tradition of Bashing 9th Circuit." *Washington Post*, last accessed April 9, 2018. Federal Judge Paul Friedman characterized Trump's comments about the judiciary as "a chief executive who criticizes virtually every judicial decision that doesn't go his way and denigrates judges who rule against him, sometimes in very personal terms. He seems to view the courts and the justice system as obstacles to be attacked and undermined, not as a coequal branch to be respected even when he disagrees with its decisions." Katie Shepard, "Trump 'violates all recognized democratic norms,' federal judge says in biting speech on judicial independence." *The Washington Post*, November 8, 2019. https://www.washingtonpost.com/nation/2019/11/08/judge-says-trump-violates-democratic-norms-judiciary-speech/, last accessed November 11, 2019. The pardons in the war crimes cases were reported in *The New York Times*. Dave Philips, "Trump Clears Three Service Members in War Crimes Cases," November 15, 2019, https://www.nytimes.com/2019/11/15/us/trump-pardons.html?action=click&module=Top%20Stories&pgtype=Homepage, last accessed November 16, 2019

Page 208... *Pentagon leaders were "fuming"*... David Ignatius, "Trump's meddling in a SEAL disciplinary case risks a collision with the Navy," The Washington Post, November 21, 2019. https://www.washingtonpost.com/opinions/trump-is-sabotaging-his-military/2019/11/21/6b46199e-0cad-11ea-97ac-a7ccc8dd1ebc_story.html, last accessed November 22, 2019. The Secretary of the Navy was fired for publicly expressing his disagreement with the president. Helene Cooper, Maggie Haberman, and Dave Philips, "Esper Demands Resignation of Navy Secretary over Seal Case," New York Times, November 25, 2019, Section A, Page 1. https://www.nytimes.com/2019/11/24/us/politics/navy-secretary-richard-spencer-resign.html?action=click&module=Top%20Stories&pgtype=Homepage, last accessed November 25, 2019.

Pages 208-209 ... *China's Chief Justice Zhou Qiang stated*...Michael Forsythe, "China's Chief Justice Rejects an Independent Judiciary and Reformers Wince," New York Times, January 19, 2017, at p. A8.

Page 209 ... *Similar attacks upon an independent court system*... *See* https://protectdemocracy.org/wp-content/uploads/2017/12/Preserving-the-Courts.pdf, last accessed November 22, 2019.

Page 209 ... *"recall" laws have been enacted* .... "Judges Shouldn't be Partisan Punching Bags," Editorial, New York Times, April

9, 2018. https://www.nytimes.com/2018/04/08/opinion/judicial-independence.html, last accessed April 9, 2018. This editorial stated that by early 2018, "lawmakers in at least 16 states are considering at least 51 bills that would diminish or politicize the role of the judiciary."

Page 209...*removed from the bench for unpopular decisions*... A recall election successfully removed Chief Judge Rose Bird of the California Supreme Court from the bench, apparently because of her "categorical opposition" to the death penalty, reflected in her vote to set the penalty aside in all 61 capital cases that came before her. https://protectdemocracy.org/wp-content/uploads/2017/12/Preserving-the-Courts.pdf, last accessed January 13, 2020.

Page 209 ...*President Bob Carlson reported*...
https://www.americanbar.org/news/abanews/aba-news-archives/2019/02/statement-of-bob-carlson--aba-president-re--undermining-judicial, last accessed December 24, 2019

Page 209 ... *operated under a random case assignment system*... Alex Botoma, Divisional Judge-Shopping, 49 Columbia Human Rights Law Review, at p. 97; see also, How Judge Shopping in Texas Led to Ruling Against Health Care Law, *New York Times*, December 25, 2018, at p. A17.

Page 210....focused solely upon...The American Bar Association Standing Committee of the Judiciary "has always evaluated only the professional competence, integrity and judicial temperament of each nominee." http://www.abanet.org/scfedjud, last accessed June 10, 2019.

Page 211 ... *picked by the Federalist Society*... A Conservative Plan to Weaponize the Federal Judiciary, *New York Times*, November 23, 2017, p. 1; Charlie Savage, Trump is Rapidly Reshaping the Judiciary. Here's How, *New York Times*, November 11, 2017, p. A1; "Counsel Quietly Trying to Corral Trump While

Pushing G.O.P.'s Agenda," *New York Times*, January 27, 2018, p. A1. The Senate confirmed a candidate for the Eighth Circuit Court of Appeals although the ABA rated him "not qualified." Thomas Kaplan, Trump is Putting Indelible Conservative Stamp of the Judiciary, *New York Times*, August 1, 2018, p. A15. In an interview with Breitbart, "Trump pledged, 'We're going to have great judges, conservative, all picked by the Federalist Society'." How the Trump Administration is Remaking the Courts, *New York Times Magazine*, August 26, 2018.

Page 211 ....*ideological credentials "central to the nominating process"*....
http://www.slate.com/articles/news_and_politics/jurisprudence/2017/01/how_the_federalist_society_became_the_de_facto_selector_of_republican_supreme.html

See, also, Linda Greenhouse, *A Conservative Plan to Weaponize the Federal Judiciary*, *New York Times*, November 23, 2017. See, also Charlie Savage, *"Trump is Rapidly Reshaping the Judiciary. Here's How," New York Times*, November 12, 2017, p. A1, and "Counsel Quietly Trying to Corral Trump While Pushing G.O.P.'s Agenda," *New York Times*, January 27, 2018, p. A1

CPSIA information can be obtained
at www.ICGtesting.com
Printed in the USA
LVHW111519190620
658098LV00007B/118/J